PACEMAKER® PRACTICAL ENGLISH SERIES

GRAMMAR MAKES SENSE

Beverley A. Dietz

A PACEMAKER® BOOK

FEARON/JANUS
Belmont, California

Simon & Schuster Supplementary Education Group

Pacemaker® Practical English Series

Grammar Makes Sense
Capitalization and Punctuation Make Sense
Writing Makes Sense
Spelling Makes Sense
Vocabulary Makes Sense

ISBN 0–8224–5101–8

Printed in the United States of America.

3 4 5 6 7 8 9 10

CO

CONTENTS

Pronouns

Adjectives and Adverbs

Conjunctions and Interjections

Prepositions

Sentence parts

Previewing SENTENCES

What is a sentence?

A sentence is a group of words that expresses a complete thought.

A SENTENCE: *We will have pizza.*

A NON-SENTENCE: *We will pizza.*

How many kinds of sentences are there?

Four: 1) declarative (makes a statement) *Pizza tastes good.*
2) interrogative (asks a question) *Do you like pizza?*
3) imperative (gives a command) *Buy me a pizza.*
4) exclamatory (expresses excitement) *I love pizza!*

How many main parts does a sentence have?

Two: 1) subject (names what the sentence is about)

The pizza parlor

2) predicate (tells something about the subject)

closes at midnight

Can a sentence have more than one subject?

Yes. This is called a compound subject.

Olives and onions are good on pizza.

Can a sentence have more than one predicate?

Yes. This is called a compound predicate.

The pizza was ordered at nine and delivered at ten.

Are some long sentences made up of two short sentences?

Yes. These are called compound sentences.

Mushroom pizza is Tom's favorite, but my favorite is pepperoni.

BEFORE STARTING THIS EXERCISE, read Grammar Rule 1 in the Reference Guide.

PRECHECK. **Read each group of words below. If the words form a complete sentence, write** *sentence* **on the line. If the words do not form a complete sentence, leave the line blank. Check your answers at the bottom of the page.**

1. The average canary has 2,200 feathers. _____

2. Groucho Marx in the movie <u>Duck Soup</u>. _____

3. People spend more money on dog food than on baby food. _____

4. Wild lions like catnip. _____

5. Will shake hands with another chimp. _____

Number right: _____ *If less than 5, review the rule in the Reference Guide.*

Read the groups of words below. Underline only the word groups that form complete sentences.

1. Most of the people in Greenland.

2. By thumping their feet.

3. Somebody sneezed.

4. Billiard balls are baked in ovens.

5. Sometimes for 15 days or more.

6. Most athletes like the color red.

7. In China, slot machines are called "hungry tigers."

8. Tight shoes make a person eat more.

9. Had been riding the roller coaster for seven hours.

10. The Egyptians made mummies out of crocodiles.

ANSWERS 1. sentence 3. sentence 4. sentence

SENTENCES/Recognizing sentences

BEFORE STARTING THIS EXERCISE, read Grammar Rule 1 in the Reference Guide.

Add one or more words to each word group below to form a complete sentence. Write your new sentence on the writing line.

1. terribly boring

   _____

2. the shock

   _____

3. at the end of a long horror movie

   _____

4. a very thirsty camel

   _____

5. had suddenly disappeared

   _____

6. a tiny tattoo

   _____

7. learning to gargle

   _____

8. no one

   _____

9. in Alaska

   _____

10. remembered my name

    _____

11. leaped over the edge

    _____

SENTENCES/Kinds of sentences

BEFORE STARTING THIS EXERCISE, read Grammar Rule 2 in the Reference Guide.

PRECHECK. Read each sentence below and decide what kind it is. Write *declarative, interrogative, imperative,* or *exclamatory* on the line next to the sentence. Check your answers at the bottom of the page.

1. Who plays shortstop on the Peanuts baseball team? _____

2. Batman graduated from Disco Tech. _____

3. Just sign the check over to me. _____

4. What kind of animal was Mr. Ed? _____

5. It's turning orange! _____

Number right: _____ *If less than 5, review the rule in the Reference Guide.*

Read each sentence below and decide what kind it is. Then write *declarative, interrogative, imperative,* or *exclamatory* on the line next to the sentence.

1. How many teeth does a shark have? _____

2. What a ridiculous suggestion that was! _____

3. Iowa got its name from an Indian word meaning "sleepy ones." _____

4. Please count them again. _____

5. Do you think you could carry a million one-dollar bills? _____

6. That's impossible! _____

7. A billion years from now, each day will be 30 hours long. _____

SENTENCES/Kinds of sentences

BEFORE STARTING THIS EXERCISE, read Grammar Rule 2 in the Reference Guide.

What kind of sentence is the woman on the left saying?
Write *declarative*, *interrogative*, *imperative*, or *exclamatory*
on the line beneath each of her sentences. What might the
man on the right reply? In each of his speech balloons, write
a short sentence of the kind indicated at the bottom of the
balloon.

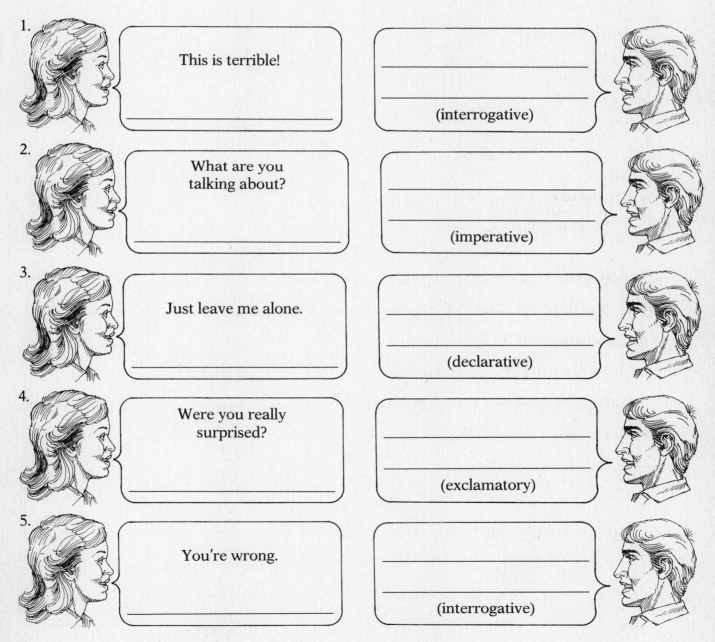

1. This is terrible!

   _____

   _____

   (interrogative)

2. What are you talking about?

   _____

   _____

   (imperative)

3. Just leave me alone.

   _____

   _____

   (declarative)

4. Were you really surprised?

   _____

   _____

   (exclamatory)

5. You're wrong.

   _____

   _____

   (interrogative)

SENTENCES/Subjects and predicates in declarative sentences

BEFORE STARTING THIS EXERCISE, read Grammar Rule 3 in the Reference Guide.

PRECHECK. **Read these declarative sentences. Part of each sentence has been underlined. On the line next to each sentence, write *subject* if the subject is underlined, or *predicate* if the predicate is underlined. Check your answers at the bottom of the page.**

1. James Bond's boss is known only as M. _____

2. Miss Moneypenny works as M's private secretary. _____

3. Caviar is one of Bond's favorite foods. _____

4. Around the corner streaks his dark blue Aston Martin. _____

5. To the rescue comes the famous hero. _____

Number right: _____ *If less than 5, review the rule in the Reference Guide.*

Read these declarative sentences. On the line next to each one, tell whether the subject or the predicate of the sentence is underlined.

1. For many years, people had known about the Arkansas cave. _____

2. The famous cave had never before been fully explored. _____

3. A group of experienced explorers volunteered. _____

4. Several reporters went to cover the event. _____

5. They followed the explorers through a lot of tunnels. _____

6. Finally, the group came to a huge cavern. _____

7. From the back of the dark cavern came a low moan. _____

8. Out of the cave raced the terrified group. _____

9. They tried to appear calm. _____

10. An alert photographer recorded their hasty exit. _____

SENTENCES/Subjects and predicates in declarative sentences

BEFORE STARTING THIS EXERCISE, read Grammar Rule 3 in the Reference Guide.

Finish each declarative sentence below by writing a subject on the blank line.

1. _____ never returned.

2. _____ learned to operate several different

   machines.

3. _____ surprised almost everybody there.

4. On the wing of the small plane struggled _____

   _____ .

5. _____ had exploded.

6. In the far corner stood _____ .

7. _____ made an important decision that

   night.

8. Over the first gate leaped _____ .

Finish each declarative sentence below by writing a predicate on the blank line.

1. Those rusty scissors _____ .

2. The most experienced detectives in the department _____

   _____ .

3. The best hot dogs _____ .

4. Most football coaches _____ .

5. A track of muddy footprints _____ .

6. Twenty-one bicycle riders _____ .

7. No one else in the whole town _____ .

8. A sudden storm _____ .

SENTENCES/Subjects and predicates in interrogative sentences

BEFORE STARTING THIS EXERCISE, read Grammar Rule 4 in the Reference Guide.

PRECHECK. Read these interrogative sentences. Part of each sentence has been underlined. On the line next to each sentence, write *subject* if the subject is underlined, or *predicate* if the predicate is underlined. Check your answers at the bottom of the page.

1. Who was the Gipper? _____

2. Which coach told his team to win for the Gipper? _____

3. Did that team actually win? _____

4. Who lost the game? _____

5. When did that famous game take place? _____

Number right: _____ *If less than 5, review the rule in the Reference Guide.*

Read these interrogative sentences. On the line next to each one, tell whether the subject or the predicate of the sentence is underlined.

1. How much does a baseball weigh? _____

2. What is the inside of a baseball made of? _____

3. How heavy should a bat be? _____

4. How long should a bat be? _____

5. Who is the game's most famous hitter? _____

6. When did the Dodgers move from Brooklyn to Los Angeles? _____

7. Which teams played in the last World Series? _____

8. Who was voted "Most Valuable Player" in that series? _____

9. Why did the Giants trade Willie Mays to New York? _____

10. Did that player really make three errors in a single inning? _____

ANSWERS 1. subject 2. subject 3. predicate 4. subject 5. predicate

SENTENCES/Subjects and predicates in imperative sentences

BEFORE STARTING THIS EXERCISE, read Grammar Rule 5 in the Reference Guide.

PRECHECK.   Read these imperative and declarative sentences. The word in parentheses after each sentence tells you what part of the sentence to write on the line. If you are to write the sentence's subject and it is understood, write *you*. Check your answers at the bottom of the page.

1. Put your hands up. *(Subject)* _____

2. Now turn around slowly. *(Predicate)* _____

3. All the cash is in that safe. *(Subject)* _____

4. Open it. *(Predicate)* _____

5. I don't know the combination *(Subject)* _____

Number right: _____ If less than 5, review the rule in the Reference Guide.

Read these imperative or declarative sentences. The word in parentheses after each sentence tells you what part of the sentence to write on the line. If you are to write the sentence's subject and it is understood, write *you*.

1. Turn to page 76. *(Predicate)* _____

2. Tear this coupon out. *(Subject)* _____

3. Fill in your name and address. *(Subject)* _____

4. Indicate the color you want. *(Predicate)* _____

5. Mail the coupon to our company. *(Subject)* _____

6. Include a check for $15.95. *(Predicate)* _____

7. Your package will arrive in six to eight weeks. *(Subject)* _____

8. Open it promptly. *(Predicate)* _____

SENTENCES/Subjects and predicates in exclamatory sentences

BEFORE STARTING THIS EXERCISE, read Grammar Rule 6 in the Reference Guide.

PRECHECK.   Read these exclamatory sentences. The word in parentheses after each sentence tells you what part of the sentence to write on the line. Check your answers at the bottom of the page.

1. I feel great today! *(Predicate)* _____

2. Nothing will help! *(Subject)* _____

3. What an awful surprise you must have had! *(Subject)* _____

4. How frightening that was! *(Predicate)* _____

5. You broke it! *(Predicate)* _____

Number right: _____ *If less than 5, review the rule in the Reference Guide.*

Read these exclamatory sentences. The word in parentheses after each sentence tells you what part of the sentence to write on the line.

1. It was a fake! *(Subject)* _____

2. What a complete disaster that was! *(Predicate)* _____

3. What dumb ideas he always has! *(Subject)* _____

4. You weren't even there! *(Predicate)* _____

5. That can't be right! *(Predicate)* _____

6. The safe is completely empty! *(Predicate)* _____

7. What a shock we had! *(Subject)* _____

8. How silly you looked! *(Predicate)* _____

9. They have disappeared! *(Subject)* _____

10. This storm may last forever! *(Predicate)* _____

SENTENCES/Subjects and predicates in sentences

BEFORE STARTING THIS EXERCISE, read Grammar Rules 3–6 in the Reference Guide.

Read each sentence below. On the line next to each one, write the subject of the sentence. If the subject is understood, write *you*.

1. Look at that lizard. _____

2. It is called a chameleon. _____

3. Have you ever seen one before? _____

4. When will the chameleon change its color? _____

5. Could those be horns on its head? _____

6. The lizard is about seven inches long. _____

7. Its tongue is as long as its body! _____

8. How does the chameleon's mouth hold such a big tongue? _____

9. Powerful throat muscles control the creature's tongue. _____

10. What an amazing animal we are looking at! _____

Read each sentence below. On the line next to each one, write the predicate of the sentence.

1. You may throw the dice first. _____

2. Are these dice loaded? _____

3. You must be kidding! _____

4. That was just a joke. _____

5. Go on and toss them. _____

6. How could you have rolled two sixes? _____

7. I did not cheat! _____

8. Give me the dice. _____

9. It is still my turn! _____

10. Go ahead, then. _____

SENTENCES/Sentences with compound subjects

BEFORE STARTING THIS EXERCISE, read Grammar Rule 7 in the Reference Guide.

PRECHECK. Read each sentence below. If it has a compound subject, write *compound* on the line next to the sentence. Then underline the subjects in the sentence. If the sentence does not have a compound subject, do not mark it. Check your answers at the bottom of the page.

1. The queen and most of her advisers were furious. _____

2. Benjamin Franklin was interested in politics, science, and philosophy. _____

3. Babe Ruth, Joe DiMaggio, and Hank Aaron were great hitters. _____

4. Buck Rogers and Killer Kane were enemies on a radio program. _____

5. Three different networks will broadcast the championship fight. _____

Number right: _____ If less than 5, review the rule in the Reference Guide.

Read each sentence below. In each sentence with a compound subject, underline the subjects. Do not mark sentences that do not have compound subjects.

1. Octopus and squid are popular foods in many parts of the world.

2. Butterflies and moths can get drunk on certain kinds of flowers.

3. Chico, Harpo, Groucho, and Zeppo became famous in vaudeville and movies.

4. Donald Duck and his family lived in Ducksburg.

5. Fleas and dogs are often found together.

6. Annie Oakley named her favorite horse Target.

7. Fingernails usually grow faster than toenails.

8. Seals, pandas, and other zoo animals need vacations from people.

9. Four other actresses had already turned down the role.

10. A famous clown and a famous bear shared the name Bozo.

SENTENCES/Sentences with compound subjects

BEFORE STARTING THIS EXERCISE, read Grammar Rule 7 in the Reference Guide.

Finish each sentence below by writing another subject on the blank line.

1. French fries and _____ are especially popular there.

2. Three scoops of coffee ice cream, two scoops of chocolate ice cream, two sliced bananas, and _____ filled the huge dish.

3. The brave sheriff and _____ finally rescued the frightened farmers.

4. Four students and _____ had argued about it for more than three hours.

5. The crowded streets, bad weather, and _____ discouraged most of the tourists.

6. The president and _____ will meet soon to discuss it.

7. That famous comedian and _____ included a very funny sketch about baseball in their act.

8. Three pencils, a test booklet, and _____ sat on every desk.

9. Soccer, football, and _____ are the most popular games in this area.

10. Sausage, green peppers, and _____ are the pizza toppings I like best.

11. Three fire engines and _____ responded to the call.

12. Penguins and _____ are natives of the polar regions.

SENTENCES/Sentences with compound predicates

BEFORE STARTING THIS EXERCISE, read Grammar Rule 8 in the Reference Guide.

PRECHECK. Read each sentence below. If it has a compound predicate, write *compound* on the line next to the sentence. Then underline the predicates in the sentence. If the sentence does not have a compound predicate, do not mark it. Check your answers at the bottom of the page.

1. The famous collector bought the only two copies of the rare stamp and then burned one of them. _____

2. The record holder first roller-skated across Canada and then rolled across the United States. _____

3. Rick Nelson began as a radio performer, then worked as a TV actor, and finally became a rock-and-roll singer. _____

4. Comedian Steve Martin wrote a book called Cruel Shoes. _____

Number right: _____ If less than 4, review the rule in the Reference Guide.

Read each sentence below. Underline the predicates in each sentence with a compound predicate. Do not mark the sentences that do not have compound predicates.

1. The famous pool player took the table and pocketed 150 consecutive balls.

2. The Shadow uncovered evil and dispensed justice.

3. The lemmings had simply followed the animal at the head of the line.

4. An Aztec king drank 50 pitchers of chilled chocolate every day.

5. Mr. Drake read the note quickly and then tore it into tiny pieces.

6. The largest lobster on record weighed 42 pounds.

7. Annie was first in a comic strip and later was the star of a movie.

SENTENCES/Sentences with compound predicates

BEFORE STARTING THIS EXERCISE, read Grammar Rule 8 in the Reference Guide.

Finish each sentence below by writing another predicate on the blank line(s).

1. The plane took off from New York at noon and _____
   _____ .

2. Everyone stopped and _____
   _____ .

3. The receiver signaled a fair catch and _____
   _____ .

4. The other players jumped off the bench, rushed onto the court, and _____
   _____ .

5. Willard baited the hook carefully, cast his line skillfully, and _____
   _____ .

6. The mysterious stranger lit a match and _____
   _____ .

7. Dina walked to the edge of the high board, looked down into the water, and _____
   _____ .

8. Miss Winters took one look at the cartoon and _____
   _____ .

9. The director turned to the audience and _____
   _____ .

10. The promoter printed 3,000 copies of the letter and _____
    _____ .

11. Somebody reached into the tourist's pocket, removed his wallet, and _____
    _____ .

SENTENCES/Compound sentences

BEFORE STARTING THIS EXERCISE, read Grammar Rule 9 in the Reference Guide.

PRECHECK. Read each sentence below. If it is a compound sentence, write *compound* on the line following the sentence. If it is not a compound sentence, leave the line blank. Check your answers at the bottom of the page.

1. I love candy, but it gives me cavities. _____

2. Claustrophobia is the fear of small places, and agoraphobia is the fear of open spaces. _____

3. At the age of 59, Satchel Paige became the oldest player in big-league baseball history. _____

4. Many golf carts are made in Poland, but there are no golf courses in that country. _____

5. Blood pressure has two measures, systolic and diastolic. _____

Number right: _____ *If less than 5, review the rule in the Reference Guide.*

Read each sentence below. Underline each compound sentence. Do not mark the sentences that are not compound.

1. A young boy released a helium-filled balloon in Dobbs Ferry, New York, and it floated all the way to a sheep ranch in Australia.

2. St. Louis and Brooklyn once played with a yellow baseball, but white has remained the official ball color.

3. Of the first five presidents of the United States, only one was not a Virginian.

4. Baseball is very popular in Japan, but football has never caught on there.

5. You can enter this huge tomato in the county fair, or you can add it to the salad.

6. A woman in Colorado crocheted a yarn chain nearly 35 miles long.

SENTENCES/Compound sentences

BEFORE STARTING THIS EXERCISE, read Grammar Rule 9 in the Reference Guide.

Use the conjunction *and, but,* or *or* to make each pair of sentences below into one sentence. Write your new sentence on the writing lines.

1. Susan Book actually works in a library. Dale Dye really is a coroner.

   _____

   _____

2. Paul Revere really did make that famous midnight ride. He billed the Massachusetts government for his expenses.

   _____

   _____

3. Ty Cobb stole 96 bases in 1915. Maury Wills finally broke Cobb's record in 1962.

   _____

   _____

4. The witnesses may have been confused. They might have been lying.

   _____

   _____

5. Farmers can now grow chickens without feathers. These birds catch cold very easily.

   _____

   _____

6. Gardenia and orange blossoms are known for their sweet smell. The two fragrances cancel each other out.

   _____

   _____

Writing Activity 1

If you need help, review page 1 and the rules noted on pages 2–17.

Part of a story is given on the right. Continue the story on the lines below. Write one or two more paragraphs, using at least three different kinds of sentences.

What a shock I had yesterday! As usual, I arrived at school just before the last bell was about to ring. I rushed to my locker, ready to grab my notebooks. I expected to see the familiar mess of gym shoes, overdue library books, and spare sweatshirts. Instead, all my belongings were stacked neatly on the locker floor or hung from hooks I had never noticed. On top of my textbooks was a small box wrapped in silver paper. Who could have been rearranging my locker? And what could possibly be inside the box?

_____

_____

_____

_____

_____

_____

_____

_____

_____

_____

_____

_____

_____

_____

_____

_____

Previewing NOUNS

What is a noun?

A noun is a word that names a person, place, or thing.

A NOUN: *hat*

How many forms does a noun have?

Most nouns have two forms: singular and plural.

1. A singular noun names *one* person, place, or thing.

   boy

2. A plural noun names more than one person, place, or thing.

   boys

What is the difference between a common noun and a proper noun?

A common noun is the name of any person, place or thing.

boy

A proper noun is the special name of a particular person, place, or thing.

Charles Johnson

What is a possessive noun?

A possessive noun shows ownership.   *the **boy's** hat*

What is a noun of address?

A noun of address names the person being spoken to.

*Where is your hat, **Charles**?*

What is an appositive noun?

An appositive noun identifies the noun that comes before it in a sentence.

*Charles, the **boy** next door, wore a new hat.*

NOUNS/Recognizing nouns

BEFORE STARTING THIS EXERCISE, read Grammar Rule 10 in the Reference Guide.

PRECHECK. Find the noun in each sentence below. Then write the noun on the line next to the sentence. Check your answers at the bottom of the page.

1. Though a penguin can swim expertly, it cannot fly. _____

2. They had not even tasted the oatmeal yet. _____

3. Most monkeys are very nearsighted. _____

4. It did not last more than four minutes. _____

5. You should have followed the directions more carefully. _____

Number right: _____ *If less than 5, review the rule in the Reference Guide.*

Underline each noun in the following sentences.

1. An average hog can oink in 20 different tones.

2. Frogs pull their eyeballs in to close their eyes.

3. Turtles are not known for their speed, but one kind of turtle can swim faster than any person can run.

4. One species of fish gulps air and then belches loudly.

5. In a typical year, a bucking bronco in a rodeo works for only ten minutes.

6. A flying fox is actually a bat.

7. Some people who fish use pink nets to attract more fish.

8. Every porcupine can float in water.

9. Although the dove is a symbol of peace, doves are actually fierce little birds.

10. A survey shows that American dogs are meaner than British dogs.

NOUNS/Using nouns

BEFORE STARTING THIS EXERCISE, read Grammar Rule 10 in the Reference Guide.

On the lines below, rewrite the paragraph given on the right. Replace each *** with a noun.

One *** and two *** made an important *** not long ago. First, they discussed their *** for many ***. Finally, they agreed on a ***. Secretly, they met in the ***. One *** poured a small *** of *** into a *** of ***. The *** flowed upward when it was poured. The *** tried their *** again, and the same *** occurred. The *** were all very excited by their ***. They called several *** and made a ***. Then they hired a *** and a ***. Now the three *** are hoping to write a *** and to appear on ***.

NOUNS/Singular and plural forms of nouns

BEFORE STARTING THIS EXERCISE, read Grammar Rule 11 in the Reference Guide.

PRECHECK. Find the plural noun in each sentence below. Write that noun on the line next to the sentence. Check your answers at the bottom of the page.

1. Who were the passengers on the Yellow Submarine? _____

2. How many different characters followed the yellow brick road to the

    Emerald City? _____

3. Where do the Jolly Green Giant and his workers live? _____

4. Which comedians starred in the movie The Silver Streak? _____

5. How many blue properties does a Monopoly board have? _____

Number right: _____ *If less than 5, review the rule in the Reference Guide.*

In the following sentences, underline each singular-form noun. Draw two lines under each plural-form noun.

1. The average eyebrow has about 550 hairs.

2. The workers who test perfumes are called "noses."

3. In almost all cases, a musician hears more clearly with the right ear than with the left ear.

4. A person who smokes usually has more wrinkles than a person who doesn't smoke.

5. The head of an average man weighs 13 pounds.

6. The right side of your face is probably more strongly developed than the left side of your face.

7. Young children usually have better hearing and better vision than adults or babies have.

8. Patients in mental hospitals almost never get headaches.

NOUNS/Spelling plural forms of nouns

BEFORE STARTING THIS EXERCISE, read Grammar Rule 12 in the Reference Guide.

PRECHECK. Finish each sentence below. Fill in the blank with the plural form of the noun given before the sentence. Check your answers at the bottom of the page.

1. marriage   That man has had an incredible number of _____ !

2. joy   At every wedding, he thinks about the _____ of married life.

3. misery   Before long, he is talking about its _____ .

4. ex-wife   A group of his _____ has even formed a club.

5. woman   Why would other _____ still take a chance on a man like that?

Number right: _____ If less than 5, review the rule in the Reference Guide.

Finish the paragraph below. In each numbered space, write the plural form of the singular noun with that number.

1. movie
2. book
3. story
4. Bean
5. Day
6. novel
7. Day
8. Wife
9. Wife
10. Ape

Many famous (1) _____ have been based on (2) _____ and (3) _____ that are not very well known. For example, the popular movie <u>Sunset Boulevard</u> was based on a short story called "A Can of (4) _____ ." The 1975 film <u>Three (5) _____ of the Condor</u> was developed from one of James Grody's (6) _____ , <u>Six (7) _____ of the Condor</u>. With a similar change in title, the 1949 film <u>A Letter to Three (8) _____</u> was based on a novel called <u>A Letter to Five (9) _____</u> . And a nearly forgotten book, <u>Monkey Planet</u>, was the basis for the 1968 movie <u>Planet of the (10) _____</u> .

NOUNS/Spelling plural forms of nouns

BEFORE STARTING THIS EXERCISE, read Grammar Rule 12 in the Reference Guide.

Rewrite the sentences below. Use the plural form of each noun in parentheses.

1. (Rabbit) can use their (ear) to keep warm.

   _____

2. (Elephant) are the only (mammal) that cannot jump.

   _____

3. (Shark) constantly grow new (tooth).

   _____

4. (Mosquito) can be more dangerous than (tarantula).

   _____

5. All (ostrich) have two (foot), each with two (toe).

   _____

6. White (flamingo) that eat shrimp soon have pink (feather).

   _____

7. (Fly) beat their (wing) about 200 (time) each second.

   _____

8. Twice as many (sheep) as (human) live in Montana.

   _____

9. (Group) of (goose) are called (gaggle).

   _____

10. Electric (eel) stun their (enemy) with (shock).

   _____

NOUNS/Proper nouns and common nouns

BEFORE STARTING THIS EXERCISE, read Grammar Rule 13 in the Reference Guide.

PRECHECK. Find the proper noun in each sentence below. Write that noun on the line. Check your answers at the bottom of the page.

1. What famous boy was raised by Kala, an ape? _____

2. Young Tarzan learned to swing through the trees. _____

3. The boy grew up in Africa. _____

4. He was the creation of writer Edgar Rice Burroughs. _____

5. The most famous actor to play the young ape-man was Johnny Weissmuller.

Number right: _____ *If less than 5, review the rule in the Reference Guide.*

In the sentences below, underline each common noun. Draw two lines under each proper noun.

1. Lizards have been credited with saving an entire crop of beets in Utah.

2. Cobras kill about 10,000 people in India every year.

3. Queen Elizabeth of England once paid a special visit to a tortoise named Tui Milala in the Tonga Islands.

4. A shopkeeper in San Angelo, Texas, used rattlesnakes to guard his store.

5. Alligators have survived in only two places in the world: the Yangtze River Valley in China and the Gulf Coast of the United States.

6. A six-foot-long poisonous snake in the Philadelphia Zoological Gardens actually bit itself to death one February.

7. Many New Yorkers say that alligators live in the sewers of Manhattan.

8. In 1964, Martin Luther King, Jr., won the Nobel Peace Prize.

NOUNS/Proper nouns

BEFORE STARTING THIS EXERCISE, read Grammar Rule 13 in the Reference Guide.

Make up a special name for the person, place, or thing in
each picture below. Write that proper noun on the line
below the picture. Remember to begin each word in the
proper noun with a capital letter.

1. _____

2. _____

3. _____

4. _____

5. _____

6. _____

7. _____

8. _____

9. _____

10. _____

NOUNS/Possessive nouns

BEFORE STARTING THIS EXERCISE, read Grammar Rule 14 in the Reference Guide.

PRECHECK. Finish each sentence below. Fill in the blank with the possessive form of the noun given before the sentence. Check your answers at the bottom of the page.

1. president   The _____ flock of sheep was supposed to help the war effort.

2. gardeners   The animals could do part of the _____ job.

3. sheep   The _____ grazing land was the White House lawn.

4. public   The _____ reaction was not very favorable.

5. Wilson   _____ favorite sheep chewed old cigar stubs.

Number right: _____ *If less than 5, review the rule in the Reference Guide.*

Underline the possessive noun in each sentence below.

1. The strange wild man of British Columbia's mountains is called the Sasquatch.

2. In the northwestern United States, the creature's name is Bigfoot.

3. The Himalayas' Abominable Snowman or Yeti is a similar creature.

4. Hunters' accounts of sightings of the creature are numerous.

5. Many people have seen the giant's huge footprints.

6. One man said he was carried to a Sasquatch family's lair in 1924.

7. In 1940, an eight-foot-tall hairy being's approach caused a Canadian family to flee its house.

8. Film shot in northern California in 1967 shows the hairy, man-like monster's upright walk.

9. People's fascination with this legendary creature continues.

NOUNS/Possessive nouns

BEFORE STARTING THIS EXERCISE, read Grammar Rule 14 in the Reference Guide.

Finish each sentence below by writing a possessive noun on the blank line.

1. _____ report to the board of directors was missing!

2. The report had already received the _____ approval.

3. _____ friends and associates looked everywhere.

4. They even checked the _____ wastebasket.

5. It was finally discovered in the _____ briefcase.

Now write ten sentences of your own. In each sentence, use the possessive noun given before the writing lines.

1. investigator's _____

_____

2. witnesses' _____

_____

3. suspect's _____

_____

4. lawyer's _____

_____

5. judge's _____

_____

6. jury's _____

_____

7. prison's _____

_____

NOUNS/Nouns of address

BEFORE STARTING THIS EXERCISE, read Grammar Rule 15 in the Reference Guide.

PRECHECK. Find the noun of address in each sentence below. Write that noun on the line next to the sentence. Check your answers at the bottom of the page.

1. Janet, Muhammad Ali is sitting near the front of the plane! _____

2. Mr. Ali, would you please fasten your seat belt now? _____

3. Thanks, Nancy, but I don't think I'll bother. _____

4. You see, ma'am, Superman doesn't need a seat belt. _____

5. Superman doesn't need an airplane, either, Mr. Ali. _____

Number right: _____ If less than 5, review the rule in the Reference Guide.

Underline the noun of address in each sentence below.

1. If the phone rings, please take a message, Mr. Bell.

2. Actually, Ms. Chanel, you should have worn a suit.

3. What was your first thought, Mr. Newton, when the apple fell on your head?

4. While you're in the kitchen, Dagwood, please make a sandwich for me, too.

5. What really happened to that cherry tree, George?

6. Be careful with that needle, Betsy.

7. This time, Abe, we'd like to hear the truth.

8. What happened to the nice guys, Mr. Durocher?

9. Aren't you afraid of snakes, Cleopatra?

10. Thank you, friends, for your kind attention.

NOUNS/Nouns of address

BEFORE STARTING THIS EXERCISE, read Grammar Rule 15 in the Reference Guide.

Look at each picture given below. What do you think the speaker might be saying? In each speech balloon, write a short sentence that the speaker might say. Use a noun of address in each of your sentences.

NOUNS/Appositive nouns

BEFORE STARTING THIS EXERCISE, read Grammar Rule 16 in the Reference Guide.

PRECHECK. Read each sentence below and underline the entire appositive. Then draw a second line under the appositive noun. Check your answers at the bottom of the page.

1. Woody Allen, a famous and talented movie director, once failed a college course in motion-picture production.

2. Hannibal Hamlin, vice president to Abraham Lincoln, died on July 4.

3. The person Fred Astaire most enjoyed dancing with was not Ginger Rogers, his famous partner.

4. The Beatles, a wildly popular group of singers from England, were paid only $2,400 for their first appearance in the United States.

5. Francis Stanley, the inventor of the "Stanley Steamer" car, died in an automobile accident.

Number right: _____ *If less than 5, review the rule in the Reference Guide.*

Underline the entire appositive in each sentence below. Then draw a second line under the appositive noun.

1. Dick Clark, the host of many rock music programs, is often called "the world's oldest teenager."

2. The secretary of transportation was Elizabeth Dole, the wife of the U.S. senator from Kansas.

3. Alfred Nobel, the founder of the Nobel Peace Prize, made a fortune by inventing and producing dynamite.

4. March 20 is the birthday of Big Bird, a star of a children's show.

5. Several commercials were made by Joe Namath, a famous quarterback.

NOUNS/Appositive nouns

BEFORE STARTING THIS EXERCISE, read Grammar Rule 16 in the Reference Guide.

Finish each sentence below by writing an appositive on the blank line.

1. Until then, no one had said anything to John, _____ _____ .

2. The caller, _____ , refused to leave a message.

3. The winner, _____ , did not want to accept the prize.

4. The other movie, _____ , turned out to be terribly boring.

5. Les finally showed the note to his uncle, _____ _____ .

6. The machine, _____ , seemed to be stuck in the middle of the road.

7. Lisa, _____ , greeted everybody at the door.

8. Nick discovered that Jay, _____ _____ , would be his opponent.

9. You should probably have spoken to Ms. Hale, _____ _____ .

10. Andrea, _____ , must have shown them where to look.

11. Two elephants, _____ , have disappeared from the zoo.

Writing Activity 2

If you need help, review page 19 and the rules noted on pages 20–32.

Finish the sentences below by writing a noun on each blank line. You may use singular forms or plural forms of common nouns. You may also use proper nouns.

1. The _____ explained their _____ to the

   other _____ of the _____ .

2. _____ was the most dangerous _____ the

   _____ had ever seen.

3. After several _____ , the _____ arrived

   safely in _____ .

4. At the _____ of the _____ ,

   _____ discovered an unusual _____ .

Choose one of the sentences you finished above. Use that sentence as the beginning of an original paragraph. Write your paragraph on the lines below.

_____

_____

_____

_____

_____

_____

_____

_____

_____

_____

_____

_____

Previewing VERBS

What is a verb?

A verb is a word that expresses action or being.

A VERB: *smile*

Do verbs change form to show differences in time?

Yes. (present tense)   *We **smile**.*

(past tense)   *We **smiled**.*

(future tense)   *We **will smile**.*

What is an action verb?

Action verbs express physical or mental action.   *We **smile**.*

What is a linking verb?

A linking verb tells what the sentence subject is or is like.

*You **are** kind.*

What is a verb phrase?

Two or more verbs work together in a verb phrase.

*She **will smile**.*

Do verbs have to agree with nouns?

Yes. One verb form agrees with singular nouns.   *He **smiles**.*

Another verb form agrees with plural nouns.   *They **smile**.*

What are the forms of the verb *be*?

The verb **be** has three present-tense forms: **is**, **are**, and **am**.

1. *He **is** funny.*
2. *They **are** funny.*
3. *I **am** funny.*

The verb **be** has two past-tense forms: **was** and **were**.

1. *She **was** funny.*
2. *They **were** funny.*

What are irregular verbs?

The past-tense form of most verbs ends in **d** or **ed**.   *They **laughed**.*

Irregular verbs change in other ways to form the past tense.

*go/**went**   think/**thought***

VERBS/Recognizing verbs

BEFORE STARTING THIS EXERCISE, read Grammar Rule 17 in the Reference Guide.

PRECHECK. Find the verb in each sentence below. Then write the verb on the line next to the sentence. Check your answers at the bottom of the page.

1. Many families listened to <u>The Lone Ranger</u> on the radio. _____

2. The Lone Ranger and his partner Tonto rescued many people. _____

3. The Lone Ranger always rode his favorite horse, Silver. _____

4. He often shouted, "Hi-yo, Silver!" _____

5. Clayton Moore played the Lone Ranger on TV. _____

Number right: _____ *If less than 5, review the rule in the Reference Guide.*

Underline the verb in each sentence below.

1. Berry Gordy, Jr., founded Motown Records.

2. The Motown studios are in Detroit, Michigan.

3. Three young women sang together as the Primettes.

4. They changed their name to the Supremes.

5. Diana Ross was the most famous Supreme.

6. Now Ross performs on her own.

7. The Primettes took their name from the Primes.

8. The Primes later became the Temptations.

9. Stevie Wonder recorded many songs with Motown Records.

10. He began his career as Little Stevie Wonder.

VERBS/Using verbs

BEFORE STARTING THIS EXERCISE, read Grammar Rule 17 in the Reference Guide.

Finish each sentence below by writing a verb on the blank line.

1. Suddenly something _____.

2. Dave _____ the door.

3. They _____ patiently for more than an hour.

4. Two snails _____ toward the other side.

5. Buster _____ at the stranger.

6. No one else _____ for the project.

7. Mark and his friends _____ the fence.

8. The car _____ to a stop.

9. Jessie _____ to her friends.

10. All the guests _____ funny red caps.

11. Nell _____ all the strawberries.

12. Cory _____ the notes into tiny pieces.

13. Without warning, the machine _____.

14. The sheriff _____ three horse thieves.

15. It still _____.

16. That dinosaur _____ a huge tail and a tiny brain.

17. Julio _____ last year.

18. I _____ everything.

19. She _____ the car on her way to work.

20. The principal _____ those students.

VERBS/Action verbs

BEFORE STARTING THIS EXERCISE, read Grammar Rule 18 in the Reference Guide.

PRECHECK. Find the action verb in each sentence below. Then write that verb on the line next to the sentence. Check your answers at the bottom of the page.

1. A famous accident occurred during a Grand National Steeplechase. _____

2. The favorite horse in the race threw its rider. _____

3. The rider of another horse also flew into the air. _____

4. This second rider landed in the saddle of the favorite horse. _____

5. The favorite and his new rider finished last in the race. _____

Number right: _____ *If less than 5, review the rule in the Reference Guide.*

Underline the action verb in each sentence below.

1. Sonja Henie skated nearly all her life.

2. She began as a very young child.

3. At the age of ten, Henie won Norway's figure-skating championship.

4. She competed in her first Winter Olympics at the age of 12.

5. Eventually, she received three Olympic gold medals.

6. Henie also won ten world figure-skating titles.

7. A famous Russian ballerina inspired Sonja Henie's work.

8. The great skater never really retired.

9. She made several movies in Hollywood.

10. People today still enjoy these movies.

VERBS/Action verbs

BEFORE STARTING THIS EXERCISE, read Grammar Rule 18 in the Reference Guide.

Finish each sentence below by writing an action verb on the blank line.

1. An expert _____ those knots.

2. Ali _____ at the strange letter.

3. No one _____ the person in the picture.

4. One of the guests _____ the silver.

5. The flame _____ .

6. The librarian _____ at three noisy men.

7. The guards _____ her camera.

8. They _____ .

9. Rico _____ about it for a long time.

10. Mr. Greenburg _____ that story.

11. Nobody _____ the changes.

12. Lila _____ the ice.

13. The boxers _____ into the ring.

14. Just before midnight, the package _____ .

15. Perhaps they _____ too many questions.

16. Someone _____ the dishwasher.

17. Jerry _____ the green pickup truck.

18. The senator actually _____ on the table.

19. The chemist _____ the foaming solution.

20. She _____ the robot to bring her slippers.

VERBS/Linking verbs

BEFORE STARTING THIS EXERCISE, read Grammar Rule 19 in the Reference Guide.

**PRECHECK. Find the linking verb in each sentence below.
Then write that verb on the line next to the sentence. Check
your answers at the bottom of the page.**

1. Dan Rowan was a host of the TV show <u>Laugh-In</u>. _____

2. Dick Martin was Rowan's partner. _____

3. Goldie Hawn and Henry Gibson were regulars on the show. _____

4. Many of the show's jokes are still funny. _____

5. Richard Nixon was once a guest on the show. _____

Number right: _____ *If less than 5, review the rule in the Reference Guide.*

**Finish each sentence below by writing a linking verb on the
blank line.**

1. You _____ too easy to fool.

2. It _____ almost impossible.

3. The first two contestants _____ very nervous.

4. I _____ absolutely sure.

5. Maybe it _____ an inside job.

6. The acrobats _____ unsteady.

7. Everyone else _____ disappointed.

8. Those lions _____ almost tame.

9. Our players _____ stronger than theirs.

10. Jennie and Todd _____ perfect for those roles.

VERBS/Verb phrases

BEFORE STARTING THIS EXERCISE, read Grammar Rule 20 in the Reference Guide.

PRECHECK. Underline the verb phrase in each sentence below. Check your answers at the bottom of the page.

1. Rock musicians have entertained people for many years now.

2. Elvis Presley's "Heartbreak Hotel" and "Hound Dog" were first recorded in 1956.

3. Chuck Berry was writing and singing rock songs in the late 1950s.

4. Rock music has always appealed especially to young people.

5. But many rock performers have been admired by older people, too.

Number right: _____ If less than 5, review the rule in the Reference Guide.

Underline the verb phrase in each sentence below.

1. For over 200 years, Americans have celebrated their independence on July 4.

2. On July 4, 1776, England's king didn't know about American independence.

3. On that day, he had noted "nothing of importance" in his diary.

4. The news from America must have surprised the king.

5. Other important events have also taken place on July 4.

6. On that day in 1817, the construction of the Erie Canal was beginning.

7. In 1848, workers were laying the cornerstone of the Washington Monument.

8. In 1862, Lewis Carroll was first telling the story "Alice in Wonderland."

9. In 1884, the United States was accepting the Statue of Liberty, a gift from France.

VERBS/Main verbs in verb phrases

BEFORE STARTING THIS EXERCISE, read Grammar Rule 20 in the Reference Guide.

Rewrite the sentences below. Replace each *** with a main verb.

1. The people in that little boat might *** help.

_____

2. Our city's hockey team has *** every game this season.

_____

3. An 18-story building could *** inside the Astrodome.

_____

4. By Monday, she had already *** her allowance.

_____

5. Only right-handed players can *** in polo matches.

_____

6. A large polar bear may *** half a ton.

_____

7. Dr. Seuss has been *** children's books since 1937.

_____

8. Even a friendly chimp can *** dangerous.

_____

9. Millions of people must have *** at Jack Benny's jokes.

_____

10. The planet Uranus was first *** George's Star.

_____

VERBS/Helping verbs in verb phrases

BEFORE STARTING THIS EXERCISE, read Grammar Rule 20 in the Reference Guide.

Rewrite the sentences below. Replace each * with one or more helping verbs.**

1. Mickey Mouse *** appearing in films since 1928.

   _____

2. Turkey Lurkey *** eaten by Foxy Loxy.

   _____

3. Uncle Scrooge McDuck *** hoarding his money.

   _____

4. Why *** Bugs Bunny always ask, "What's up, Doc?"

   _____

5. Miss Piggy *** become famous for asking, "Moi?"

   _____

6. Mr. Ed, a famous horse, *** talk.

   _____

7. Sylvester the Cat *** always chasing Tweetybird.

   _____

8. What *** Jungle Jim name his pet monkey?

   _____

9. Why *** Superman name his pet monkey Beppo?

   _____

10. Everybody *** searching for the missing dog, Spot.

    _____

VERBS/Using verb phrases

BEFORE STARTING THIS EXERCISE, read Grammar Rule 20 in the Reference Guide.

On the lines below, rewrite the paragraph given on the right. Replace each *** with a verb phrase.

Mr. Thompson *** a bad day. It was only ten o'clock, and already nearly a dozen things *** wrong. First, his alarm clock *** , and then his coffee maker *** . Then the shower *** and the sink *** . While backing his car out of the garage, poor Mr. Thompson *** two garbage cans and a mailbox. Then he *** in traffic for almost an hour. Naturally, he *** late for work, and his boss *** for him. Just as Mr. Thompson *** down at his desk, his telephone *** . The company president *** for three important memos that Thompson *** last week. Mr. Thompson could only wish that he *** in bed.

VERBS/Agreement of verbs with nouns

BEFORE STARTING THIS EXERCISE, read Grammar Rule 21 in the Reference Guide.

PRECHECK. Decide which of the verb forms in parentheses should be used to finish each sentence below. Then write that verb form on the line next to the sentence. Check your answers at the bottom of the page.

1. Elmer J. Fudd always (wear, wears) red shoes. _____

2. Monty Python's Big Red Book (have, has) a blue cover. _____

3. Many people still (remember, remembers) the Red Baron. _____

4. Red Skelton's fans all (know, knows) Freddie the Freeloader. _____

5. Charlie Brown (have, has) a crush on the little red-haired girl. _____

Number right: _____ If less than 5, review the rule in the Reference Guide.

Finish each sentence below. Select the correct verb form from the pair given before the sentence. Then write that verb form on the blank line.

1. steal, steals   Some bees _____ honey from other bees.

2. walk, walks   Most polar bears never _____ on dry land.

3. paint, paints   Blue satin bower birds _____ the insides of their nests.

4. swims, swim   Most whales _____ about four miles an hour.

5. run, runs   An angry pig _____ 11 miles an hour.

6. cough, coughs   Many fish _____ in dirty water.

7. scares, scare   Deep water sometimes _____ birds.

8. lay, lays   The average hen _____ 227 eggs every year.

9. helps, help   Male and female robins _____ each other with their young.

10. has, have   Rattlesnakes _____ forked tongues.

VERBS/Agreement of verbs with nouns

BEFORE STARTING THIS EXERCISE, read Grammar Rule 21 in the Reference Guide.

Rewrite the sentences below. Replace each *** with a present-tense verb. Be sure your verb agrees with the subject of the sentence.

1. Most people *** science fiction movies.

   _____

2. Not all beavers *** dams.

   _____

3. The president *** everyone else what to do.

   _____

4. Jason *** every morning.

   _____

5. Her parents *** three newspapers every day.

   _____

6. Mosquitoes usually *** men.

   _____

7. Their cat *** more than 20 pounds.

   _____

8. This train *** at every little town along the way.

   _____

9. That program *** too many commercials.

   _____

10. In my opinion, too many people *** .

   _____

VERBS/Agreement of verbs with compound subjects

BEFORE STARTING THIS EXERCISE, read Grammar Rule 22 in the Reference Guide.

PRECHECK. Decide which of the verb forms in parentheses should be used to finish each sentence below. Then write that verb form on the line next to the sentence. Check your answers at the bottom of the page.

1. Snoopy and his brother Spike (come, comes) from the Daisy Hill Puppy Farm. _____

2. Tom and Jerry (chases, chase) each other in cartoons. _____

3. Ernie and Bert (live, lives) on Sesame Street. _____

4. Archie and Jughead (goes, go) to Riverdale High School. _____

5. Beanie and Cecil (has, have) a friend named Tear-Along, the Dotted Lion. _____

Number right: _____ *If less than 5, review the rule in the Reference Guide.*

Finish each sentence below. Select the correct verb form from the pair given before the sentence. Then write that verb form on the blank line.

1. appear, appears   Mary Richards and her friends still _____ in TV reruns.

2. explore, explores   In other reruns, Captain Kirk and his crew _____ space in their ship.

3. lives, live   Beaver and Wally Cleaver and their parents still _____ in Mayfield.

4. avoid, avoids   Mr. and Mrs. Wilson _____ their next-door neighbor, Dennis.

5. works, work   Adam, Hoss, and Little Joe still _____ with their father on the ranch.

6. patrol, patrols   Officer Toody and Officer Muldoon _____ the neighborhood in Car 54.

7. picks, pick   Fred Flintstone and Charley _____ up boulders at the Rockhead and Quarry Construction Company.

VERBS/Agreement of verbs with compound subjects

BEFORE STARTING THIS EXERCISE, read Grammar Rule 22 in the Reference Guide.

Rewrite the sentences below. Replace each *** with a present-tense verb. Be sure your verb agrees with the compound subject.

1. Donkeys and rabbits *** long ears.

   _____

2. The students and their teacher *** about that.

   _____

3. Our neighbor and her brother *** old cars.

   _____

4. A hippo and a hummingbird *** in that movie.

   _____

5. Three parakeets and a canary *** in the same cage.

   _____

6. Johnny Carson and Ed McMahon *** many late-night fans.

   _____

7. That film critic and his partner *** in a TV show.

   _____

8. The book and the movie *** different endings.

   _____

9. Barb and Ken *** pet crickets.

   _____

10. Those cats and that dog *** almost all the time.

   _____

VERBS/Forms of the verb *be*

BEFORE STARTING THIS EXERCISE, read Grammar Rule 23 in the Reference Guide.

PRECHECK. Decide which of the verb forms in parentheses should be used to finish each sentence below. Then write that verb form on the line next to the sentence. Check your answers at the bottom of the page.

1. I (are, am) still a fan of the old TV show, <u>Father Knows Best.</u> _____

2. The father in the show (was, were) Jim Anderson. _____

3. His three children (was, were) Betty, Bud, and Kathy. _____

4. His special name for Betty (was, were) Princess. _____

5. TV shows today (is, are) not usually as good as old reruns. _____

Number right: _____ *If less than 5, review the rule in the Reference Guide.*

Finish each sentence below. Select the correct verb form from the pair given before the sentence. Then write that verb form on the blank line.

1. was, were   Superman's first home _____ the planet Krypton.

2. was, were   His name there _____ Kal-El.

3. was, were   His next home _____ Smallville, Illinois.

4. was, were   His adoptive parents _____ John and Martha Kent.

5. was, were   The Kents _____ happy to have such a powerful son.

6. is, are, am   All the <u>Superman</u> movies _____ very popular.

7. is, are, am   Christopher Reeve _____ the star of the current <u>Superman</u> movies.

8. is, are, am   Lois Lane _____ Superman's girlfriend.

9. is, are, am   Phone booths _____ some of Superman's dressing rooms.

10. is, are, am   I _____ still a fan of the old <u>Superman</u> comic books.

ANSWERS 1. am 2. was 3. were 4. was 5. are

VERBS/Forms of the verb *be*

BEFORE STARTING THIS EXERCISE, read Grammar Rule 23 in the Reference Guide.

Rewrite the sentences below. Replace each *** with a present-tense form of the verb *be*.

1. Actor Larry Hagman *** Mary Martin's son.

   _____

2. Singers Crystal Gayle and Loretta Lynn *** sisters.

   _____

3. Fang *** not the real name of Phyllis Diller's husband.

   _____

4. Warren Beatty and Shirley MacLaine *** brother and sister.

   _____

   _____

Rewrite the sentences below. Replace each *** with a past-tense form of the verb *be*.

1. Captain Bob and Princess Summer-Fall-Winter-Spring *** stars of The Howdy Doody Show.

   _____

   _____

2. Fidel Castro *** once a guest on an American TV show.

   _____

3. John Dillinger *** the first Public Enemy Number One.

   _____

4. Annette, Bobby, and Tim *** three of the original Mouseketeers.

   _____

   _____

BEFORE STARTING THIS EXERCISE, read Grammar Rule 24 in the Reference Guide.

Finish each sentence below. Fill in the blank with the correct form of the verb given before the sentence.

1. grow   Last year they _____ 15 different vegetables.

2. sing   Reg _____ three solos in yesterday's concert.

3. tell   You must have _____ somebody else.

4. throw   She should not have _____ the ball to Kyle.

5. ride   Jeff _____ a horse for the first time last week.

6. swim   Gina _____ on the team last year.

7. know   Until now, no one else _____ the secret.

8. fall   Two skiers _____ in yesterday's race.

9. go   Ella _____ to Mexico last winter.

10. ride   We have never _____ an elephant before.

11. fall   Eight inches of snow had _____ during the night.

12. sing   They had never _____ in front of an audience before.

13. go   Everyone else has _____ to the movies.

14. grow   That plant has _____ nearly a foot in the past month.

15. tell   Jay _____ us the same story last week.

16. swim   I had never _____ that far before.

17. know   Tina and Rita have _____ each other for many years.

18. throw   Someone _____ a rock through that window this morning.

19. bite   Judy was _____ by a spider the other day.

20. steal   The diamond necklace had been _____ a month earlier.

VERBS/Irregular verbs

BEFORE STARTING THIS EXERCISE, read Grammar Rule 24 in the Reference Guide.

Finish each sentence below. Fill in the blank with the correct form of the verb given before the sentence.

1. drink   Our family _____ 30 gallons of milk last month.

2. give   The movie had _____ everyone a creepy feeling.

3. fly   The pilot has never _____ this plane before.

4. begin   Last season, all the games _____ on time.

5. break   Before that accident, Todd had never _____ any bones.

6. do   Well, you _____ the best you could yesterday.

7. run   More than 2,000 people _____ in the marathon last weekend.

8. drive   They _____ from Florida to Alaska last summer.

9. write   Last month, Mom _____ five letters to the newspaper.

10. give   Nobody _____ me any presents on my last birthday.

11. run   He has _____ in every election since 1964.

12. begin   That group has finally _____ to sing well together.

13. drink   Alice had _____ a cup of strange medicine.

14. write   The author had never _____ a play before.

15. break   Someone _____ my favorite record last night.

16. drive   None of us had ever _____ such a big truck before.

17. fly   Last time, the plane _____ above the clouds.

18. do   No one else has ever _____ it that well.

19. blow   Last night, Grandpa _____ out all the candles on his cake.

20. ring   The phone had _____ 12 times before I reached it.

VERBS/Irregular verbs

BEFORE STARTING THIS EXERCISE, read Grammar Rule 24 in the Reference Guide.

**Finish each sentence below. Fill in the blank with the correct
form of the verb given before the sentence.**

1. see   The witness had _____ the thief entering the building.

2. bring   You should have _____ your notes along.

3. choose   Lynn should have _____ the prize behind Door Number 2.

4. steal   Somebody _____ five cars from our neighborhood last night.

5. take   Jenna _____ her first skating lesson last week.

6. buy   After three hours of shopping, we still hadn't _____ anything.

7. catch   After the swimming party, most of the guests _____ colds.

8. tear   Just before he left, Jake _____ three pages out of his notebook.

9. eat   Someone had already _____ all the pizza.

10. steal   She has never _____ anything in her life.

11. bring   Sam _____ two dates to the party last night.

12. take   He has already _____ up too much of our time.

13. tear   I have already _____ your note into tiny pieces.

14. eat   Rob _____ spinach for the first time last night.

15. see   Annette has _____ that movie 11 times.

16. wear   Ray had never _____ such heavy boots before.

17. buy   Lisa _____ herself a new sports car last Saturday.

18. forget   He has _____ today's appointment.

Writing Activity 3

If you need help, review page 34 and the rules noted on pages 35–52.

Look at the picture given on the right.

List at least four verbs that might help you to tell about the man's actions.

_____

_____

Think about what might have happened to the man, and about what he might do next. Now write a short story about the man in the picture. Be sure to use all of the verbs you noted above to help you describe the man's actions.

_____

_____

_____

_____

_____

_____

_____

_____

_____

_____

Previewing PRONOUNS

What is a personal pronoun?

A personal pronoun is a word that takes the place of one or more nouns.

A PERSONAL PRONOUN: *she*

Do personal pronouns have different forms?

Yes. Each personal pronoun has a subject form and an object form.

SUBJECT FORM: *She hit the ball.*

OBJECT FORM: *The ball hit her.*

What is the antecedent of a pronoun?

The antecedent is the noun that the pronoun refers to.

Shelly hit the ball. Then she ran toward first base.

Do pronouns have to agree with verbs?

Yes. Singular pronouns agree with one verb form.

He plays baseball.

Plural pronouns agree with another verb form.

They play baseball.

What is an indefinite pronoun?

An indefinite pronoun refers to a general group. It has no specific antecedent.

Nobody wants to play centerfield

What is a possessive pronoun?

A possessive pronoun shows ownership.   *That bat is mine.*

What is a reflexive pronoun?

The reflexive pronoun refers back to a noun or pronoun in the same sentence.

Mary should buy herself a new glove.

What is a demonstrative pronoun?

A demonstrative pronoun points out one or more people or things.

Whose glove is that?

PRONOUNS/Recognizing personal pronouns

BEFORE STARTING THIS EXERCISE, read Grammar Rule 25 in the Reference Guide.

PRECHECK. Find the personal pronoun in each sentence below. Then write the personal pronoun on the line next to the sentence. Check your answers at the bottom of the page.

1. This game is hard to learn, but it can be a lot of fun. _____

2. I started playing with Ted last summer. _____

3. He has been playing the game for years. _____

4. At first, we had a little trouble with the rules. _____

5. Before long, you will be an expert, too. _____

Number right: _____ *If less than 5, review the rule in the Reference Guide.*

Underline each personal pronoun in the sentences below.

1. In Omaha, Nebraska, you will break the law if you sneeze in church.

2. If a woman in Florida breaks more than three dishes a day, she is breaking the law.

3. People eating rattlesnake meat in public may not know that they are breaking the law in Kansas.

4. I have heard that a law in Youngstown, Ohio, prohibits riding on the roof of a taxi.

5. When a man in Maine walks down the street with untied shoelaces, he is breaking the law.

6. Children in Missouri break the law every time they play hopscotch on a Sunday afternoon.

7. Whenever you slap a friend on the back, you are breaking a law in Georgia.

PRONOUNS/Using personal pronouns

BEFORE STARTING THIS EXERCISE, read Grammar Rule 25 in the Reference Guide.

Look at each picture given below. What do you think the speaker might be saying? In each speech balloon, write a short sentence that the speaker might say. Begin each sentence with one of these personal pronouns: *I, we, you, he, she, it, they.*

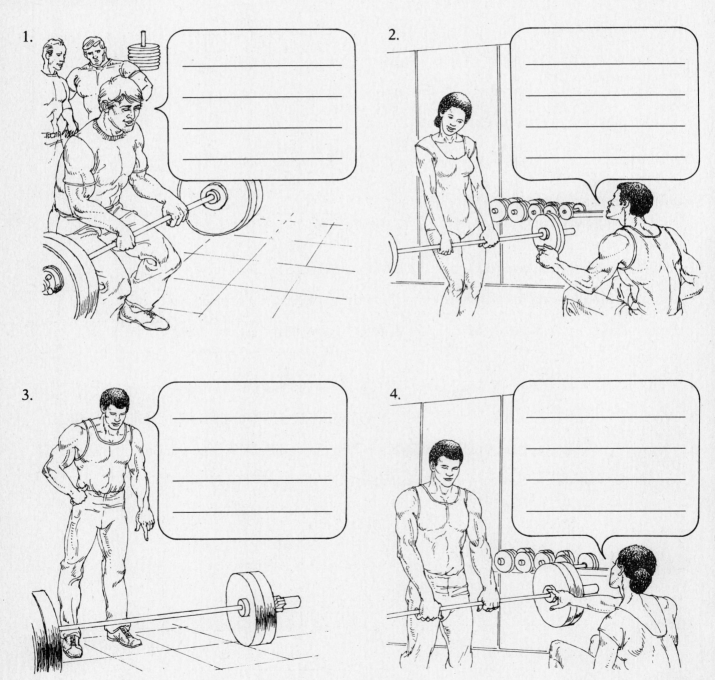

PRONOUNS/Subject forms and object forms of personal pronouns

BEFORE STARTING THIS EXERCISE, read Grammar Rule 26 in the Reference Guide.

PRECHECK. In the sentences below, underline each subject-form pronoun. Draw two lines under each object-form pronoun. Check your answers at the bottom of the page.

1. I stared at the catcher for a long time.

2. He was giving me a very clear signal.

3. Unfortunately, I could not remember the meaning of that signal.

4. Soon the fans started shouting at us.

5. They were waiting for the next pitch.

Number right: _____ If less than 5, review the rule in the Reference Guide.

Underline the personal pronoun in each sentence below. Then decide whether the pronoun is in the subject form or the object form. Write *subject* or *object* on the line next to the sentence.

1. We usually feel a little nervous around snakes. _____

2. However, they are very rarely dangerous. _____

3. I know a woman who trains snakes. _____

4. She claims that some snakes are actually friendly. _____

5. These snakes want people to like them. _____

6. One snake follows her everywhere. _____

7. She once gave a snake to a good friend. _____

8. He was quite surprised by the present. _____

9. No one had ever given him a snake before. _____

10. The man built a house for the snake so it would have a quiet place to curl up in. _____

_____

_____

PRONOUNS/Subject forms and object forms of personal pronouns

BEFORE STARTING THIS EXERCISE, read Grammar Rule 26 in the Reference Guide.

Rewrite the sentences below. Replace each *** with the subject form of a personal pronoun.

1. *** raced home and telephoned the police.

_____

2. " *** probably won't believe this," *** said.

_____

3. "My friends and *** are telling the truth, though," *** continued.

_____

4. " *** happened right outside the town hall," *** said.

_____

5. After a moment *** answered, " *** was afraid *** might ask that."

_____

Rewrite the sentences below. Replace each *** with the object form of a personal pronoun.

1. Several people stopped *** on the street.

_____

2. They all asked *** about the strange costume.

_____

3. "I don't think it looks so odd," Lee told *** .

_____

4. Most people were polite, but one man was rude to *** .

_____

5. Lee said to *** , "If you don't like *** , don't look at *** ."

_____

PRONOUNS/Antecedents of pronouns

BEFORE STARTING THIS EXERCISE, read Grammar Rule 27 in the Reference Guide.

PRECHECK. Underline the personal pronoun in each sentence below. Then write the antecedent of that pronoun on the line next to the sentence. Check your answers at the bottom of the page.

1. When Pelé began playing professional soccer, he was 15 years old. _____

2. That game was once very popular, but nobody plays it anymore. _____

3. The children began a game of tug-of-war, and several adults soon joined them. _____

   _____

4. Ali promised to win the match in the fourth round, and he did. _____

5. Janet Guthrie became famous when she drove in the Indianapolis 500. _____

Number right: _____ *If less than 5, review the rule in the Reference Guide.*

**Underline the personal pronoun in each sentence below.
Then circle the antecedent of that pronoun.**

1. Colonel Sanders became rich when he sold his fried-chicken company.

2. Although this product looks like food, it is not made to be eaten.

3. Those cows recently performed in Moscow, where they danced and
   played football.

4. Many patients start to get better when someone comes to visit them.

5. Judy Garland was 17 when she starred in The Wizard of Oz.

6. Tomatoes are popular now, but they were once considered poisonous.

7. The artist had made an important mistake, but nobody noticed it.

8. The wife of a famous poet became famous when she wrote the book
   Frankenstein.

PRONOUNS/Antecedents of pronouns

BEFORE STARTING THIS EXERCISE, read Grammar Rule 27 in the Reference Guide.

Rewrite the sentences below. Replace each * with a subject-form pronoun that goes with the underlined antecedent.**

1. <u>Scientists</u> have already made artificial bacon, and now *** are trying to produce fake steaks.

   _____

   _____

2. <u>Sue</u> had hoped to win, but *** was disappointed.

   _____

3. <u>My friends and I</u> feel discouraged, but *** do not feel defeated.

   _____

   _____

4. When my <u>brother</u> opened the box, *** fainted.

   _____

Rewrite the sentences below. Replace each * with an object-form pronoun that goes with the underlined antecedent.**

1. <u>Jack</u> told the story again, but no one believed ***.

   _____

2. Al called <u>Jim and me</u> and apologized to ***.

   _____

3. Rita fed the <u>horses</u>, but she forgot to give *** water.

   _____

4. Our family gets that <u>newspaper</u>, but no one ever reads ***.

   _____

   _____

PRONOUNS/Subject-verb agreement with personal pronouns

BEFORE STARTING THIS EXERCISE, read Grammar Rule 28 in the Reference Guide.

PRECHECK. Decide which of the verb forms in parentheses should be used to finish each sentence below. Then write that verb form on the line next to the sentence. Check your answers at the bottom of the page.

1. He usually (do, does) an outstanding job. _____

2. It (take, takes) a long time, though. _____

3. We always (admire, admires) the results. _____

4. She (feel, feels) a little jealous. _____

5. I certainly (understand, understands) her feelings. _____

Number right: _____ *If less than 5, review the rule in the Reference Guide.*

Finish each sentence below. Select the correct verb form from the pair given before the sentence. Write that verb form on the blank line.

1. are, is
She _____ the captain of our team of detectives.

2. consider, considers
When the team is on a case, it _____ every possible clue.

3. seem, seems
Sometimes it _____ as if all the clues lead nowhere.

4. explain, explains
I am the officer who _____ each new case to the detectives.

5. make, makes
One detective always _____ valuable suggestions for solving a case.

6. discuss, discusses
We _____ his suggestions with the captain.

7. know, knows
You _____ how difficult those discussions can be.

PRONOUNS/Subject-verb agreement with personal pronouns

BEFORE STARTING THIS EXERCISE, read Grammar Rule 28 in the Reference Guide.

Finish each sentence below by writing the present-tense form of a verb on the blank line. Be sure the verb agrees with the subject of the sentence.

1. They _____ tennis every weekend.

2. She _____ most of their arguments.

3. We _____ that show every week.

4. I _____ science fiction movies.

5. It _____ too much noise.

6. You _____ a good sense of humor.

7. He _____ too much.

8. I _____ almost every day.

9. Actually, we _____ it.

10. Every Saturday morning, he _____ his yard.

11. They usually _____ several parties in December.

12. She _____ five times every week.

13. You _____ better this morning.

14. It _____ to me.

15. Now he _____ the factory.

16. It usually _____ about an hour.

17. We always _____ first.

18. They _____ to the beach every summer.

19. She _____ for two hours every evening.

20. He _____ so professionally!

PRONOUNS/Indefinite pronouns

BEFORE STARTING THIS EXERCISE, read Grammar Rule 29 in the Reference Guide.

PRECHECK. Find the indefinite pronoun in each sentence below. Then write that pronoun on the line. Check your answers at the bottom of the page.

1. The explorers packed everything into their boat. _____

2. They didn't forget anything important. _____

3. Last week, someone got a message from them. _____

4. Since then, though, no one has heard from them. _____

5. Perhaps something has gone wrong! _____

Number right: _____ If less than 5, review the rule in the Reference Guide.

Each sentence below is missing an indefinite pronoun. Choose an indefinite pronoun from the list on the left to complete each sentence. Don't use any one pronoun more than once.

all
anyone
anything
everyone
everything
few
many
one
nobody
no one
nothing
several
some
someone
something

1. We were surprised that _____ went wrong.

2. Perhaps _____ else saw the accident.

3. _____ knows more about cars than I do.

4. _____ strange is going on here!

5. _____ of the speakers were boring.

6. Please tell us _____ you know about spiders.

7. He says he doesn't know _____ about it.

8. Does _____ have a volleyball to bring?

9. _____ are called, but few are chosen.

10. _____ knows the troubles I've seen.

PRONOUNS/Indefinite pronouns

BEFORE STARTING THIS EXERCISE, read Grammar Rule 29 in the Reference Guide.

On the lines below, rewrite the paragraphs given on the right. Replace each * with an indefinite pronoun.**

"Is *** ready?" the captain asked.

"Absolutely," her assistant answered. "We'll be landing on Pluto within the hour. *** could possibly go wrong now."

"Still, *** is bothering me," the captain replied. "Has *** touched these dials?"

"Of course not," the assistant said firmly. " *** is allowed in the control room except the two of us."

Just then, they both heard *** squeak. Could *** else be in the control room after all?

_____

_____

_____

_____

_____

_____

_____

_____

_____

_____

_____

_____

_____

_____

PRONOUNS/Subject-verb agreement with indefinite pronouns

BEFORE STARTING THIS EXERCISE, read Grammar Rule 30 in the Reference Guide.

PRECHECK. Decide which of the verb forms in parentheses should be used to finish each sentence below. Then write that verb form on the line next to the sentence. Check your answers at the bottom of the page.

1. For some reason, everything (look, looks) different now. _____

2. Nobody (sounds, sound) quite the same, either. _____

3. Nothing (is, are) in quite the right place. _____

4. Several of them (acts, act) just a little nervous. _____

5. Something (seems, seem) out of balance. _____

Number right: _____ If less than 5, review the rule in the Reference Guide.

Finish each sentence below. Select the correct verb form from the pair given before the sentence. Write that verb form on the blank line.

1. have, has   Unfortunately, no one in the group _____ a better suggestion.

2. is, are   Everyone else _____ ready now.

3. stays, stay   Nothing _____ the same.

4. enjoys, enjoy   Almost everybody _____ these old movies.

5. knows, know   Several of those gorillas _____ sign language.

6. makes, make   Nothing in this story really _____ sense.

7. likes, like   Of course, nobody _____ waiting in line.

8. pounds, pound   Suddenly, someone _____ on the door.

9. goes, go   Many of the sailors _____ wild on shore leave.

10. winds, wind   Some of them even _____ up in jail.

PRONOUNS/Subject-verb agreement with indefinite pronouns

BEFORE STARTING THIS EXERCISE, read Grammar Rule 30 in the Reference Guide.

Finish each sentence below by writing the present-tense form of a verb on the blank line. Be sure the verb agrees with the subject of the sentence.

1. Nobody _____ harder than Sally.

2. Now everyone _____ your idea.

3. Something exciting _____ every night.

4. Most of his friends _____ he's crazy.

5. This time, everybody _____ three guesses.

6. Anything _____ more sense than that.

7. Nothing ever _____ here.

8. After most lectures, no one _____ any questions.

9. Everybody _____ the same thing.

10. Several of the whales _____ through hoops of fire.

11. Nothing _____ to Karl.

12. Everyone still _____ a little tired.

13. Everything _____ for at least five minutes.

14. Someone still _____ in that old building.

15. Everybody _____ that mistake at least once.

16. Some of those medicine bottles _____ broken seals.

17. Now somebody _____ every call.

18. No one else _____ .

19. Nothing _____ me when I'm asleep.

20. Almost everyone _____ taxes.

PRONOUNS/Possessive pronouns

BEFORE STARTING THIS EXERCISE, read Grammar Rule 31 in the Reference Guide.

PRECHECK. Find the possessive pronoun in each sentence below. Then write that pronoun on the line next to the sentence. Check your answers at the bottom of the page.

1. Can a leopard change its spots? _____

2. Why don't bees bend their knees? _____

3. Is that cat wearing my hat? _____

4. Does the puppy fetch his pipe and slippers? _____

5. Is that pet snake really yours? _____

Number right: _____ *If less than 5, review the rule in the Reference Guide.*

Underline the possessive pronoun in each sentence below.

1. The people in a New York crowd clapped their hands for over 50 hours.

2. A California man set a record by beating his drums for over 42 days.

3. Two Seattle girls set their own record by playing hopscotch for 1,200 hours.

4. An Indiana student is proud to point out that the tallest house of cards in the world is his.

5. Fourteen students traveled 602 miles by leapfrogging over their fraternity brothers.

6. A woman in England set a record by rocking in her rocking chair for more than 400 hours.

7. A Frenchman broke his own record by eating 15 pounds of bike parts.

8. A couple of trapeze artists were married 60 feet above the crowd during their circus performance in Houston.

ANSWERS 1. its 2. their 3. my 4. his 5. yours

67

PRONOUNS/Possessive pronouns

BEFORE STARTING THIS EXERCISE, read Grammar Rule 31 in the Reference Guide.

Rewrite the sentences below. Replace each *** with a possessive pronoun.

1. Angie was trying to open *** locker.

   _____

2. "Why is *** locker door stuck?" she wondered.

   _____

3. Then *** friend Tim walked up to the locker next to ***.

   _____

   _____

4. He opened *** locker and took out *** books.

   _____

5. Then he looked at Angie strangely and asked, "Are you sure that's *** locker?"

   _____

   _____

6. "Of course," she answered. "I know what *** locker looks like."

   _____

   _____

7. Tim pointed to Brad and said, "Angie, I think that locker is ***."

   _____

   _____

8. Angie looked again at the locker she thought was ***. Then she sheepishly said, "I do know what *** locker looks like. But this one isn't ***."

   _____

   _____

PRONOUNS/Reflexive pronouns

BEFORE STARTING THIS EXERCISE, read Grammar Rule 32 in the Reference Guide.

PRECHECK. Find the reflexive pronoun in each sentence below. Then write that pronoun on the line next to the sentence. Check your answers at the bottom of the page.

1. W. C. Fields invented hundreds of false names for himself. _____

2. Thieves had helped themselves to all the best jewelry. _____

3. You were obviously only thinking of yourself. _____

4. Unfortunately, the computer cannot fix itself. _____

5. That famous artist often uses herself as a model. _____

Number right: _____ If less than 5, review the rule in the Reference Guide.

Finish each sentence below by writing a reflexive pronoun on the line.

1. We will have to finish the wallpapering by _____ .

2. The lawyer represented _____ at the trial.

3. Cats usually keep _____ quite clean.

4. I could swear that this door just opened by _____ .

5. Those parachutists might have hurt _____ .

6. I'm going to treat _____ to a double banana split.

7. Apparently, the actress chose the new stage name by _____ .

8. The doctor had tried to cure _____ .

9. If you three want sauerkraut, you'll have to cook it _____ .

10. Which job to take is a decision you'll have to make for _____ .

PRONOUNS/Demonstrative pronouns

BEFORE STARTING THIS EXERCISE, read Grammar Rule 33 in the Reference Guide.

PRECHECK. Find the demonstrative pronoun in each sentence below. Then write that pronoun on the line next to the sentence. Check your answers at the bottom of the page.

1. This might be a funny new television show. _____

2. It has a lot in common with these. _____

3. That didn't happen by chance. _____

4. Those were all very successful. _____

5. The new show's producers are surely aware of that. _____

Number right: _____ *If less than 5, review the rule in the Reference Guide.*

Finish each sentence below by writing a demonstrative pronoun on the blank line.

1. Staring at all the work on my desk, I said, " _____ is ridiculous!"

2. Then my boss walked over with a thick file and said, " _____ will be your next project."

3. I pointed to the dozen other files on my desk and asked, "But what about _____ ?"

4. " _____ will just have to wait," she told me.

5. She continued with, "You had better get right to work on _____ ."

6. " _____ is what you said about the other files," I reminded her.

7. " _____ were all very important yesterday," my boss replied.

8. "Now," she explained, " _____ is your only important project."

9. "OK," I said, "then _____ is what I'll work on next."

10. My boss left and I thought, "Now _____ is even more ridiculous!"

Writing Activity 4

If you need help, review page 54 and the rules noted on pages 55–70.

The picture given below shows Kay and Ray having an argument. The beginning of their conversation is given on the right. Read what Kay and Ray have said to each other so far, and underline the eight pronouns they have used. Then finish their argument on the writing lines. Use at least three different kinds of pronouns in your part of the conversation.

Ray: Look, this just isn't fair! I don't think you know what you are doing.

Kay: Actually, I don't care about your opinion. Everything doesn't always have to be done your way.

Ray: _____
_____
_____

Kay: _____
_____
_____

Ray: _____
_____
_____

Kay: _____
_____
_____

Ray: _____
_____
_____

Kay: _____
_____
_____

Previewing ADJECTIVES

What is an adjective?

An adjective is a word that adds to the meaning of a noun or pronoun.

AN ADJECTIVE: *red* apple

Which adjectives are called indefinite articles?

The indefinite articles are **a** and **an**.

an apple   *a* basket of apples

What is a predicate adjective?

A predicate adjective adds to the meaning of the subject noun or pronoun. It comes after the linking verb.

All the apples in the basket were ***ripe***.

What is a proper adjective?

A proper adjective is formed from a proper noun.

Washington *apples*

What is the comparative form of an adjective?

The comparative form of an adjective compares two people or things.

This apple is big, but that apple is ***bigger***.
These apples are delicious, but those are ***more delicious***.
Their apples are good, but our apples are ***better***.

What is the superlative form of an adjective?

The superlative form of an adjective compares more than two people or things.

This is the ***juiciest*** *apple of all.*
She grew the ***most delicious*** *apples.*
That is the ***worst*** *apple I ever tasted.*

ADJECTIVES/Recognizing adjectives

BEFORE STARTING THIS EXERCISE, read Grammar Rules 34 and 35 in the Reference Guide.

PRECHECK. Find the adjective in each sentence below. Then write the adjective on the line next to the sentence. Check your answers at the bottom of the page.

1. Doctors are considered truthful people. _____

2. Ancient Egyptians slept on pillows of stone. _____

3. Rickshaws were invented by an American. _____

4. Benjamin Franklin drew political cartoons. _____

5. Brave explorers climbed Mount Everest. _____

Number right: _____ *If less than 5, review the rules in the Reference Guide.*

Underline each adjective in the sentences below. (Ignore the article *the*.)

1. Silver dollars were the first coins made in the United States.

2. At one time the fashionable women of Japan blackened their teeth.

3. The life of an average fly lasts two weeks.

4. The first abacus was used in Egypt, not China.

5. The male cricket produces a greater number of chirps in warm weather.

6. Rubber is an essential ingredient of some gum.

7. The cast of the movie included those eight lions.

8. Some giant tortoises live to an age of 200 years.

9. Nearly every adult in Iceland can read and write.

10. Black sheep have a better sense of smell than white sheep have.

ADJECTIVES/Using adjectives

BEFORE STARTING THIS EXERCISE, read Grammar Rules 34 and 35 in the Reference Guide.

Rewrite the sentences below. Replace each *** with an adjective.

1. The *** girl won *** prize in the *** contest.

_____

_____

2. The *** author once wrote *** stories for *** *** magazine.

_____

_____

3. The *** athletes smiled winningly at the *** judges.

_____

_____

4. A thousand pounds of *** *** seed were delivered to the *** farmer.

_____

_____

5. The *** painting caused a *** stir among *** *** critics.

_____

_____

6. Those *** and *** tiger cubs crawled all over their *** mother.

_____

_____

7. The *** *** player won a *** amount of money *** year.

_____

_____

ADJECTIVES/Using adjectives

BEFORE STARTING THIS EXERCISE, read Grammar Rule 34 in the Reference Guide.

On the lines below, rewrite the paragraphs given on the right. Whenever you see the adjective *nice*, replace it with an adjective that gives a clearer description.

The candidate, dressed in a nice suit, stood up on the nice platform. "Thank you! Thank you!" the candidate shouted. "I want to thank all of you nice voters. Without you, I would not have been elected governor of this nice state. Of course, I also want to thank all the nice members of my staff—especially my nice campaign manager. I'd like to thank these nice members of the press, too."

Then the candidate pointed to a nice man in the front row of the crowd. "Most of all," the candidate continued, "I want to thank my nice psychiatrist for all his nice support."

_____

_____

_____

_____

_____

_____

_____

_____

_____

_____

_____

_____

_____

_____

_____

_____

_____

ADJECTIVES/The adjectives *a* and *an*

BEFORE STARTING THIS EXERCISE, read Grammar Rule 35 in the Reference Guide.

PRECHECK. In each sentence below, decide whether *a* or *an* should be used in place of the ***. Then write *a* or *an* on the line next to the sentence. Check your answers at the bottom of the page.

1. Sarah Bernhardt was *** famous actress. _____

2. After *** operation, she performed with a wooden leg. _____

3. Bernhardt had *** unusually long career. _____

4. She also managed *** theater in Paris. _____

5. The "Divine Sarah" sometimes slept in *** coffin. _____

Number right: _____ *If less than 5, review the rule in the Reference Guide.*

Finish the sentences below by writing *a* or *an* on each blank line.

1. With its tail off the ground, _____ kangaroo cannot jump.

2. _____ average porcupine has more than 30,000 quills.

3. _____ group of hogs is called _____ herd.

4. Ivory may come from the tusks of _____ elephant, _____ boar, or _____ walrus.

5. _____ squirrel sees everything in black and white.

6. _____ old male monkey may have _____ bald head.

7. _____ hippopotamus can run faster than _____ human.

8. The eohippus, _____ ancestor of the horse, was no bigger than _____ average dog.

9. _____ sea lion on board _____ ship may become seasick.

10. _____ hornbill is a large bird that has _____ enormous bill.

ADJECTIVES/Predicate adjectives

BEFORE STARTING THIS EXERCISE, read Grammar Rule 36 in the Reference Guide.

PRECHECK. Find the predicate adjective in each sentence below. Then write that adjective on the line next to the sentence. Check your answers at the bottom of the page.

1. Honeybees are deaf. _____

2. Shrimp are actually quite noisy. _____

3. All jaguars are afraid of dogs. _____

4. Bald eagles are not really bald. _____

5. Certain sharks are hungry all the time. _____

Number right: _____ *If less than 5, review the rule in the Reference Guide.*

Underline the predicate adjective in each sentence below.

1. Steve McPeak has become famous as a daredevil.

2. McPeak's exploits can be very risky.

3. His tightrope walk over Yosemite Valley was fantastic!

4. As a child, McPeak was afraid of heights.

5. Now heights and danger are very exciting for him.

6. McPeak sounds casual about his records.

7. Other people are quite impressed by his stunts.

8. McPeak is not foolish, however.

9. Even for this daredevil, some stunts are too dangerous.

10. So although he may seem crazy, McPeak has his own safety standards.

ADJECTIVES/Predicate adjectives

BEFORE STARTING THIS EXERCISE, read Grammar Rule 36 in the Reference Guide.

Rewrite the sentences below. Replace each *** with a predicate adjective.

1. Their music was too ***.

   _____

2. All the other contestants seemed terribly ***.

   _____

3. Large doses of table salt can be ***.

   _____

4. A good friend should be ***.

   _____

5. The end of the game was rather ***.

   _____

6. Naturally, most of the soldiers were ***.

   _____

7. The builders were extremely *** of their work.

   _____

8. No one else seemed *** about the results.

   _____

9. Suddenly, the crowd became ***.

   _____

10. The instructions for that game are too ***.

    _____

11. This mission may be very ***.

    _____

ADJECTIVES/Proper adjectives

BEFORE STARTING THIS EXERCISE, read Grammar Rule 37 in the Reference Guide.

PRECHECK. Find the proper adjective in each sentence below. Then write that adjective on the line next to the sentence. Check your answers at the bottom of the page.

1. One English queen spent her entire life in Italy. _____

2. Many cities have Mardi Gras festivals in late winter. _____

3. At one time, any Russian man with a beard had to pay a special tax. _____

4. A Roman emperor once made his horse a senator. _____

5. Samuel Morse invented the telegraph and Morse code. _____

Number right: _____ *If less than 5, review the rule in the Reference Guide.*

Underline each proper adjective in the sentences below.

1. That family owns a German sedan and a Japanese pickup.

2. A Chinese typewriter has as many as 5,700 characters.

3. France is actually the country where Scottish kilts were first worn.

4. The Navajo tribe is the largest tribe of Indians in the United States.

5. In 1939, George VI became the first British king to visit the United States.

6. Have you read the latest Stephen King book?

7. In a famous game of championship Ping-Pong, a Polish player and a Rumanian player volleyed for more than two hours on the opening serve.

8. Ancient Greek boxers began every match by touching noses.

9. Can you name the last Hawaiian king?

ADJECTIVES/Proper adjectives

BEFORE STARTING THIS EXERCISE, read Grammar Rule 37 in the Reference Guide.

Finish the sentences below by writing a proper adjective on each blank line.

1. There are more than a dozen _____ restaurants in the _____ district of the city.

2. I wish I could go on a _____ cruise.

3. The _____ tourists were overwhelmed by all the traffic in that _____ city.

4. Jerome added _____ cheese and _____ olives to the salad.

5. The _____ holiday is one of my favorites.

6. A _____ satellite orbited the moon.

7. The _____ and _____ teams will play for the ice-hockey championship.

8. During the entire battle, only one _____ soldier and two _____ soldiers were wounded.

9. Have you seen the latest _____ film at the Bijou?

10. Three _____ scientists performed the experiments together.

11. Alexandre-Gustave Eiffel designed the famous _____ landmark.

12. That bank was financed with _____ money.

13. I'm going to a resort over the long _____ weekend.

14. That _____ song always makes me smile.

15. Her _____ uniform was actually quite flattering.

ADJECTIVES/Comparative forms of adjectives

BEFORE STARTING THIS EXERCISE, read Grammar Rule 38 in the Reference Guide.

PRECHECK. Decide which form of the adjective in parentheses should be used to finish each sentence below. Then write that adjective form on the line next to the sentence. Check your answers at the bottom of the page.

1. The sequel will be even (good) than the original movie. _____

2. Hot water is (heavy) than cold water. _____

3. A crocodile may be (dangerous) than a lion. _____

4. Michael Jackson is (young) than his brother Tito. _____

5. Your idea was even (bad) than mine! _____

Number right: _____ If less than 5, review the rule in the Reference Guide.

Finish each sentence below. Select the correct form of the adjective given before the sentence. Then write that adjective form on the blank line.

1. famous   Charlie Brown is _____ than most real people.

2. short   No other pro baseball player was _____ than Eddie Gaedel.

3. colorful   Most landscapes are _____ in the summer than they are in the winter.

4. happy   The loser looked _____ than the winner.

5. good   No other toothpaste does a _____ job than Glitz.

6. high   A child's temperature should be _____ than an adult's.

7. bad   This stew tastes even _____ than the last batch you made!

8. popular   Dogs are _____ pets than snakes.

9. silly   That comedian is _____ than any other comedian on TV.

10. beautiful   That house is so much _____ now that it has been fixed up.

ADJECTIVES/Superlative forms of adjectives

BEFORE STARTING THIS EXERCISE, read Grammar Rule 38 in the Reference Guide.

PRECHECK. Decide which form of the adjective in parentheses should be used in each sentence below. Then write that adjective form on the line next to the sentence. Check your answers at the bottom of the page.

1. South Point High in Calcutta, India, is the (large) school in the world.

   _____

2. Rolls Royces are among the (expensive) cars in the world. _____

3. The 1903 World Series, with a total of 33 errors, may have been the

   (bad) series in history. _____

4. Jupiter is by far the (big) planet in our solar system. _____

5. Of all dogs, the greyhound has the (good) eyesight. _____

Number right: _____ If less than 5, review the the rule in Reference Guide.

Finish each sentence below. Fill in the blank with the correct form of the adjective given before the sentence.

1. rich   As a young actress, Shirley Temple was probably the

   _____ child in the world.

2. expensive   The _____ strawberries in the world cost $42 apiece.

3. successful   Clint Eastwood is one of Hollywood's _____ actors.

4. accurate   The _____ clock in the world is in the town hall of
                  Copenhagen, Denmark, and it never shows the wrong time.

5. terrible   An Italian train tunnel was the scene of one of history's

                  _____ railroad accidents.

6. effective   Aspirin is still one of the _____ painkillers on the
                  market.

ADJECTIVES/Comparative and superlative forms of adjectives

BEFORE STARTING THIS EXERCISE, read Grammar Rule 38 in the Reference Guide.

Rewrite each sentence below. Use the correct form of the adjective in parentheses.

1. You are (tall) in the morning than you are at night.

2. A certain ranch in Texas is (big) than the entire state of Rhode Island.

3. The world's (long) escalator is in Moscow, U.S.S.R.

4. A Ping-Pong ball is (heavy) than a hummingbird's nest.

5. The Panama Canal is the (busy) ship canal in the world.

6. The world's (big) toy store is in London, England.

7. A short tongue twister may be (difficult) than a long one.

Previewing ADVERBS

What is an adverb?

An adverb is a word that adds to the meaning of a verb or verb phrase. Adverbs usually tell four things.

WHEN	*left **early***	HOW	*sang **sweetly***
WHERE	*went **outside***	HOW OFTEN	*called **twice***

What is the comparative form of an adverb?

The comparative form of an adverb compares two people or things.

*Pat left **earlier** than Jay did.*

*Lisa sings **more sweetly** than Sherry does.*

*Bill called **more often** than Tom did.*

What is the superlative form of an adverb?

The superlative form of an adverb compares more than two people or things.

*Of all the men, Rob ran the **fastest**.*

*Ann learned languages the **most easily**.*

*Of all the new employees, Kate adjusted **best**.*

What is a negative adverb?

A negative adverb changes the meaning of the verb or verb phrase in a sentence.

*Fred did **not** call Dan.*

*Teresa **never** eats sweets.*

*Paul could **barely** hear Ed's voice.*

ADVERBS/Recognizing adverbs

BEFORE STARTING THIS EXERCISE, read Grammar Rule 39 in the Reference Guide.

PRECHECK. Find the adverb in each sentence below. Then write that adverb on the line next to the sentence. Check your answers at the bottom of the page.

1. Some birds can fly backward. _____

2. Yo-yos were first used as weapons. _____

3. Both contestants stepped forward. _____

4. The moon may once have been part of the earth. _____

5. Murray drummed his fingers impatiently. _____

Number right: _____ *If less than 5, review the rule in the Reference Guide.*

Underline each adverb in the sentences below.

1. Babe Ruth first became famous as a pitcher.

2. Later, he gained fame as a slugger.

3. Ruth occasionally made funny remarks about baseball.

4. Babe Ruth's record for most home runs in a season was finally broken by Roger Maris.

5. The crowd cheered wildly for the new record holder.

6. People usually give Abner Doubleday credit for inventing baseball.

7. Actually, Doubleday probably never played the game.

8. A form of baseball called rounders was originally played in England.

9. In that game, fielders deliberately tried to hit runners with the ball.

10. Happily, the game is now played differently.

ADVERBS/Using adverbs

BEFORE STARTING THIS EXERCISE, read Grammar Rule 39 in the Reference Guide.

Rewrite the sentences below. Replace each *** with an adverb.

1. Our school had a talent contest ***.

   _____

2. The first contestant stepped *** onto the stage.

   _____

   _____

3. For several minutes, he stared *** at the audience.

   _____

   _____

4. When he *** began to sing, he sang quite ***.

   _____

   _____

5. The second contestant sang the same song, but performed it pretty ***.

   _____

   _____

6. ***, the third contestant's routine used the music of the same song.

   _____

   _____

7. Everyone cheered *** when the fourth contestant appeared.

   _____

   _____

8. ***, she was a juggler who didn't use any music at all.

   _____

   _____

ADVERBS/Comparative forms of adverbs

BEFORE STARTING THIS EXERCISE, read Grammar Rule 40 in the Reference Guide.

PRECHECK. Decide which form of the adverb in parentheses should be used in each sentence below. Then write that adverb form on the line next to the sentence. Check your answers at the bottom of the page.

1. A grown dog can bark (fiercely) than a puppy. _____

2. An eagle flies (quickly) than a butterfly. _____

3. Cirrus clouds float (high) in the sky than stratus clouds. _____

4. At night, a cat can see (well) than a dog. _____

5. A woman's heart beats (fast) than a man's heart. _____

Number right: _____ If less than 5, review the rule in the Reference Guide.

Finish each sentence below. Fill in the blank with the correct form of the adverb given before the sentence.

1. slowly   A racing man runs _____ than a charging rhinoceros.

2. hard   The right lung works _____ than the left lung.

3. clearly   John Hancock signed the Declaration of Independence _____ than anyone else.

4. well   At the beginning of a game, a basketball player can hear _____ than at the end of the game.

5. often   Snow falls _____ in Maine than in Florida.

6. enthusiastically   Soccer fans cheer _____ than tennis fans.

7. easily   You can train a chimpanzee _____ than you can train a duck.

8. swiftly   A rabbit can run _____ than a mouse.

ADVERBS/Superlative forms of adverbs

BEFORE STARTING THIS EXERCISE, read Grammar Rule 40 in the Reference Guide.

PRECHECK. Decide what form of the adverb in parentheses should be used in each sentence below. Then write that adverb form on the line next to the sentence. Check your answers at the bottom of the page.

1. Of all kinds of birds, the whooper swan flies (high). _____

2. Of all kinds of birds, the horned sungem beats its wings (fast). _____

3. Of all kinds of birds, the condor beats its wings (slowly). _____

4. Of all kinds of birds, the emperor penguin dives (deep). _____

5. Of all kinds of birds, the seaside sparrow is seen (rarely). _____

Number right: _____ *If less than 5, review the rule in the Reference Guide.*

Finish each sentence below. Fill in the blank with the correct form of the adverb given before the sentence.

1. clearly   Because its theme was the best developed, that story made its point

    _____ .

2. fast   Among all birds, the ostrich runs _____ .

3. hard   Of all the batters in this game, Jerry hit the ball _____ .

4. good   Of all the players, he can pitch _____ .

5. badly   Of the 30 children in the nursery school, Timmy behaved

    _____ .

6. long   Of all these cut flowers, the orchid will last _____ .

7. well   Of the seven people who tried out for the part, you danced

    _____ .

ADVERBS/Comparative and superlative forms of adverbs

BEFORE STARTING THIS EXERCISE, read Grammar Rule 40 in the Reference Guide.

Finish each sentence below. Fill in the blank with the correct form of the adverb given before the sentence.

1. slowly   Of all land mammals, the three-toed sloth moves _____ .

2. slowly   Of course, a snail moves even _____ than a three-toed sloth.

3. long   An elephant usually lives _____ than a whale.

4. fast   Dirty snow melts _____ than clean snow does.

5. brightly   Even when it is full, the moon shines _____ than the sun.

6. recently   Of all the children in the nursery school, the baby was born

   _____ .

7. swiftly   Of all the top-notch women competing in the race, the winner

   ran _____ .

8. quickly   Any rabbit, even a very young one, moves _____ than any turtle.

9. safely   You can travel _____ if you buckle your seat belt before you begin your car trip.

10. well   Of our last four presidents, he speaks _____ .

11. often   We see people riding bicycles _____ than we see people riding unicycles or tricycles.

12. well   Most of the actors performed _____ during the dress rehearsal than they did on opening night.

ADJECTIVES AND ADVERBS/Using adjectives and adverbs

BEFORE STARTING THIS EXERCISE, *read Grammar Rule 41 in the Reference Guide.*

PRECHECK. Decide which of the words in parentheses should be used to finish each sentence below. Then write that word on the line next to the sentence. Check your answers at the bottom of the page.

1. (Actual, Actually), not all spiders spin webs. _____

2. A spider bite can be (dangerous, dangerously). _____

3. A housefly has a (soft, softly) mouth. _____

4. Some bees can sting (repeated, repeatedly). _____

5. A tarantula can be a (safe, safely) pet. _____

Number right: _____ *If less than 5, review the rule in the Reference Guide.*

Finish each sentence below. Select the correct word from the pair given before the sentence. Then write that word on the blank line.

1. brave, bravely   Several _____ swimmers walked toward the lake.

2. loud, loudly   The hard snow crunched _____ under their feet.

3. Silent, Silently   _____ , the swimmers got ready to go into the water.

4. icy, icily   One jumped into the _____ water.

5. slow, slowly   Another walked _____ into the lake.

6. nervous, nervously   Two swimmers stared _____ at the photographers.

7. warm, warmly   Most of the reporters stayed inside the _____ boathouse.

ADJECTIVES AND ADVERBS/Using adjectives and adverbs

BEFORE STARTING THIS EXERCISE, read Grammar Rule 41 in the Reference Guide.

Rewrite the sentences below. Replace each *** with an adjective. Replace each +++ with an adverb.

1. A *** stranger pushed the door +++.

   _____

2. Two *** dogs barked +++ at every passerby.

   _____

3. A *** guard stood +++ behind the gate.

   _____

4. +++, the *** crowd moved down the street.

   _____

5. The *** worker kicked the machine +++.

   _____

6. The hostess smiled +++ at her *** guests.

   _____

7. The *** students sighed +++.

   _____

8. The *** coach yelled +++ at the referee.

   _____

9. +++, a *** explosion rocked the lab.

   _____

10. That *** company treats its employees +++.

   _____

ADVERBS/The adverb *not*

BEFORE STARTING THIS EXERCISE, read Grammar Rule 42 in the Reference Guide.

PRECHECK.   Add the adverb *not* to each sentence below to change the meaning of the verb phrase. You may have to add a helping verb when you add *not*. Write your new sentence on the writing line. Check your answers at the bottom of the page.

1. Jellyfish are really fish. _____

2. Snakes feel slimy. _____

3. Falling cats always land on their feet.

   _____

4. Porcupines are able to shoot their quills.

   _____

5. Flying fish really fly. _____

Number right: _____ *If less than 5, review the rule in the Reference Guide.*

Add the adverb *not* to each sentence below to change the meaning of the verb phrase. You may have to add a helping verb when you add *not*. Write your new sentence on the writing line.

1. Toads give warts to humans. _____

2. Man-eating plants exist. _____

3. Pigs are dirty animals. _____

4. A person's hair will turn white overnight.

   _____

5. Many blackbirds have black feathers. _____

ADVERBS/Avoiding double negatives

BEFORE STARTING THIS EXERCISE, read Grammar Rule 43 in the Reference Guide.

PRECHECK. Decide whether each sentence below contains a double negative. If it does, cross out one of the negative words. If the sentence does not have a double negative, write *OK* on the line next to the sentence. Check your answers at the bottom of the page.

1. None of the weather reports had predicted snow. _____

2. Hardly nobody was prepared for the storm. _____

3. People shouldn't never have gone out in that weather. _____

4. Fortunately, there were no serious accidents. _____

5. Barely none of the town's schools and businesses were open that week. _____

Number right: _____ *If less than 5, review the rule in the Reference Guide.*

Finish each sentence below. Select the correct words from the pair given before the sentence. Write that word on the blank line. Be sure to avoid double negatives.

1. any, no — A few cats don't have _____ hair at all.

2. never, ever — Crows hardly _____ fly in a straight line.

3. can, can't — No opossum _____ really hang by its tail.

4. a, no — An elephant isn't afraid of _____ mouse.

5. hardly, really — Bats aren't _____ blind.

6. never, ever — You shouldn't _____ lift a rabbit by its ears.

7. actually, hardly — A vampire bat doesn't _____ suck blood.

8. any, no — Fleas don't have _____ wings.

9. do, don't — No flying lizards really _____ fly.

10. anywhere, nowhere — Polar bears don't go _____ in the winter.

93

ADVERBS/Avoiding double negatives

BEFORE STARTING THIS EXERCISE, read Grammar Rule 43 in the Reference Guide.

**Rewrite each sentence below. Use only one negative word
in each new sentence.**

1. A centipede doesn't really have no 100 legs.

   _____

2. Bats don't actually carry no bedbugs.

   _____

3. Snakes don't have no ears.

   _____

4. Nobody has ever seen no penguins at the North Pole.

   _____

5. Birds aren't never frightened by scarecrows.

   _____

6. You shouldn't trust no groundhogs on February 2.

   _____

7. Goats don't really eat no tin cans.

   _____

8. Bulls can't never see red because they're color-blind.

   _____

9. Camels don't really store no water in their humps.

   _____

10. Most gorillas aren't really hardly dangerous.

    _____

ADVERBS/Adverbs used as intensifiers

BEFORE STARTING THIS EXERCISE, read Grammar Rule 44 in the Reference Guide.

PRECHECK. Find the adverb used as an intensifier in each sentence below. Then write that adverb on the line next to the sentence. Check your answers at the bottom of the page.

1. In the 1970s, pet rocks made a businessman quite successful. _____

2. During the 1930s, people rather bravely swallowed goldfish. _____

3. Most puzzlers work extremely hard to solve Rubik's Cube. _____

4. The hula hoop became unusually popular in the late 1950s. _____

5. Scrabble has remained very popular for many years. _____

Number right: _____ *If less than 5, review the rule in the Reference Guide.*

Underline each adverb used as an intensifier in the sentences below.

1. In 1986, Halley's Comet came unusually close to the earth.

2. An extremely large watermelon won the blue ribbon.

3. That sculpture is a simply magnificent piece of work.

4. That rather expensive hospital was built to care for camels.

5. Your story is totally unbelievable!

6. Almost accidentally, the scientist had invented safety glass.

7. The Open University offers several rather unusual classes.

8. The two lab workers had made a very foolish mistake.

9. She is an extraordinarily beautiful woman.

10. He was barely recognizable after his face-lift.

ANSWERS 1. quite 2. rather 3. extremely 4. unusually 5. very

ADVERBS/Adverbs used as intensifiers

BEFORE STARTING THIS EXERCISE, read Grammar Rule 44 in the Reference Guide.

The list on the left below contains adverbs commonly used as intensifiers. Choose an adverb from that list to replace each *** in the paragraph given on the right. Then rewrite the paragraph on the lines at the bottom of the page. Try not to use any intensifying adverb more than once.

almost	quite
considerably	rather
exceptionally	somewhat
extremely	terribly
highly	unusually
incredibly	very

Elvis Presley was an *** popular singer during the 1950s and 1960s. After the release of his famous song "Heartbreak Hotel," Presley became a star *** immediately. Soon, he was appearing on television shows and making *** successful movies. Presley became *** wealthy, and he seemed to enjoy spending his money. He bought an *** large house that he named "Graceland." Presley filled the house with a *** large collection of statues. He filled the garage with a *** expensive collection of cars and trucks. When Presley wasn't singing or acting, he could often be seen driving *** happily down the back roads of Tennessee.

Writing Activity 5

If you need help, review pages 72 and 84 and the rules noted on pages 73–96.

Look at the picture given on the right.

Now list three adjectives that describe the people in the picture.

_____   _____   _____

List three adverbs that describe the actions of the people in the picture.

_____   _____   _____

Now write a paragraph telling what the people in the picture are doing. Use the adjectives and adverbs noted above to make your paragraph clear, colorful, and interesting.

_____

_____

_____

_____

_____

_____

_____

_____

_____

_____

97

Previewing CONJUNCTIONS

What is a coordinating conjunction?

A coordinating conjunction is a word used to join two equal parts of a sentence.

> James brought the lunch, **and** Ben brought the dinner.
>
> He remembered the forks, **but** he forgot the spoons.
>
> Janet will make lemonade **or** buy some at the store.

What is a subordinating conjunction?

A subordinating conjunction is a word used to begin an adverb clause.

> **after** we drove to the park
>
> **unless** it rains
>
> **when** the picnic begins
>
> **if** we go swimming
>
> **while** they play ball
>
> **when** we go home

CONJUNCTIONS/Coordinating conjunctions

BEFORE STARTING THIS EXERCISE, read Grammar Rule 45 in the Reference Guide.

PRECHECK. Find the coordinating conjunction in each sentence below. Then write that conjunction on the line next to the sentence. Check your answers at the bottom of the page.

1. Dorothy and her friends met the Cowardly Lion on the road to Oz. _____

2. Did Peter Sellers make movies about a red lion or about a pink panther? _____

3. Buster Brown and his friendly dog Tige lived in a shoe. _____

4. In the Captain Marvel comics, Tawny was a tiger, but he wore people's clothes. _____

5. Did the Hungry Tiger appear in the Oz books or in the Winnie-the-Pooh books? _____

Number right: _____ *If less than 5, review the rule in the Reference Guide.*

Underline the coordinating conjunction in each sentence below.

1. Huey, Dewey, and Louie are Donald Duck's nephews.

2. Lassie was the star of the show, but her friend Pokey also had many fans.

3. Superman had a dog named Krypto and a horse named Comet.

4. Mickey Mouse's dog was first called Rover, but now he is known as Pluto.

5. Who hops down the bunny trail, Crusader Rabbit or Peter Cottontail?

6. Two famous detectives, Nick and Nora Charles, had a dog named Asta.

7. Tom Terrific and Mighty Manfred were popular cartoon characters.

8. Did Batman drive the batmobile, or was that Robin's job?

9. Robin Hood and his merry band lived in Sherwood Forest.

CONJUNCTIONS/Coordinating conjunctions

BEFORE STARTING THIS EXERCISE, read Grammar Rule 45 in the Reference Guide.

Rewrite the sentences below. Replace each * with a coordinating conjunction.**

1. Reg *** Ann talked about it for hours, *** they could not agree.

_____

_____

2. You can do it my way, *** you can make your own mistakes.

_____

_____

3. Five explorers *** 52 sled dogs finally reached the South Pole.

_____

_____

4. Goats, sheep, *** cattle have horns, *** deer have antlers.

_____

_____

5. Robert Fulton improved steamboats, *** he did not actually invent them.

_____

_____

6. A fresh egg may be white, brown, *** speckled.

_____

_____

7. The storm killed seven people *** destroyed crops throughout the state.

_____

_____

CONJUNCTIONS/Subordinating conjunctions

BEFORE STARTING THIS EXERCISE, read Grammar Rule 46 in the Reference Guide.

PRECHECK. Underline the subordinating conjunction in each sentence below. Check your answers at the bottom of the page.

1. A British soldier became separated from his troops when World War I began.

2. Because she wanted to help him, a Frenchwoman hid him in her closet.

3. The soldier stayed in that closet until the war was over.

4. While he hid, German soldiers sometimes sat just a few feet away.

5. The British soldier must have felt very nervous whenever he heard the enemy soldiers.

Number right: _____ If less than 5, review the rule in the Reference Guide.

Underline the subordinating conjunction in each sentence below.

1. The three American astronauts grew taller while they traveled in space.

2. From 1912 to 1918, the U.S. Treasury washed, dried, and ironed dirty dollar bills because money was in short supply.

3. Now, dollar bills are burned whenever they become too dirty or ragged.

4. Although he had to campaign from a jail cell, Eugene V. Debs won nearly a million votes in the presidential election of 1920.

5. Before standard time was established, the United States had more than 80 different time zones.

6. One Civil War hero was only 20 when he became a Union Army general.

7. Wherever you travel, you will probably hear someone say "OK."

CONJUNCTIONS/Subordinating conjunctions

BEFORE STARTING THIS EXERCISE, read Grammar Rule 46 in the Reference Guide.

Rewrite the sentence below. Replace each *** with a subordinating conjunction.

1. Many girls started practicing gymnastics *** they wanted to be like Mary Lou Retton.

   _____

   _____

2. *** San Francisco started running cable cars, several other big cities tried these special trains.

   _____

   _____

3. *** Jack the Ripper became very famous, he was never caught.

   _____

   _____

4. Benjamin Franklin took a great risk *** he flew his kite during an electric storm.

   _____

   _____

5. *** you live in a big city, you probably walk much faster than a person from a small town.

   _____

   _____

6. The pigeons in New York's Central Park get nervous *** they hear barking dogs or moving trains.

   _____

   _____

Previewing INTERJECTIONS

What is an interjection?

An interjection is a word that simply expresses emotion. It is separated from the rest of the sentence by a comma or an exclamation point.

Oh! There's a firefly!

Hah! That's a likely story.

Oh, I like that song.

Ouch! That hurt!

Wow! You won the prize.

Ah, I'm glad to be home.

INTERJECTIONS/Using interjections

BEFORE STARTING THIS EXERCISE, read Grammar Rule 47 in the Reference Guide.

PRECHECK. Find the interjection in each sentence below.
Then write that interjection on the line next to the sentence.
Check your answers at the bottom of the page.

1. Wow! Look at that list of flavors! _____

2. Oh, they don't have my favorite. _____

3. Well, I guess I'll try the chunky bubble gum ice cream. _____

4. So, how does it taste? _____

5. Yuk! It's awful! _____

Number right: _____ *If less than 5, review the rule in the Reference Guide.*

Finish each sentence below by writing an interjection on the blank line.

1. _____ ! Watch out!

2. _____ , I think it's getting worse.

3. _____ ! They've landed!

4. _____ , maybe she changed her mind.

5. _____ , it probably won't matter anyway.

6. _____ ! Isn't that terrific?

7. _____ , please be more careful next time.

8. _____ ! That really hurts!

9. _____ , you don't really mean that, do you?

10. _____ ! Why did I do that?

INTERJECTIONS/Using interjections

BEFORE STARTING THIS EXERCISE, read Grammar Rule 47 in the Reference Guide.

Look at each picture given below. What do you think the speaker might be saying? In each speech balloon, write a short sentence that the speaker might say. Begin each sentence with an interjection.

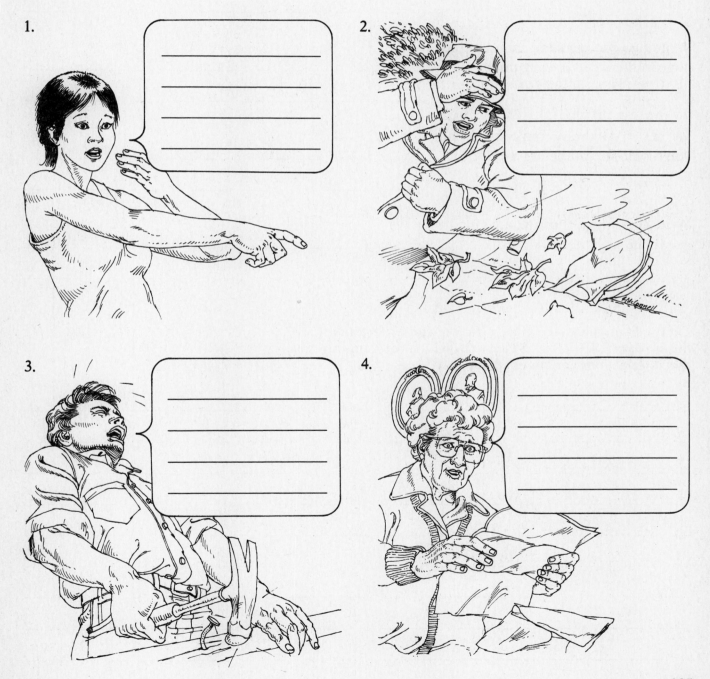

1.

2.

3.

4.

Writing Activity 6

If you need help, review pages 98 and 103 and the rules noted on pages 99–105.

Think of an argument you would like to have.

What is the name of the person you would argue with?

_____

What one or two things would you argue about?

_____

_____

Write two coordinating conjunctions you would use in the argument.

_____

_____

Write two subordinating conjunctions you would use in the argument.

_____

_____

Write two interjections you would use in the argument.

_____

_____

On the lines below, write the dialogue you expect might occur in your argument. Be sure to include the conjunctions and interjections you noted above.

_____

_____

_____

_____

_____

_____

_____

_____

Previewing PREPOSITIONS

What is a preposition?

A preposition is a word that shows the relationship of a noun or a pronoun to some other word in a sentence.

> *The lamp is **on** the table.*
> *The couch is **against** the wall.*

What is a prepositional phrase?

A prepositional phrase is a group of words that includes the preposition and the noun or pronoun that follows it.

> ***with a tablecloth***   ***over the door***

What is the object of a preposition?

The object of a preposition is the noun or pronoun that follows it.

> *of the **kitchen***   *upon the **counter***

How are personal pronouns used in prepositional phrases?

A personal pronoun that is the object of a preposition must be in the object form.

> *painted by **them***   *designed for **her***

How is a prepositional phrase used as an adjective?

A prepositional phrase is used as an adjective when it adds to the meaning of a noun or pronoun.

> *Mr. Smith **from the carpet store***
> *the fabric sample **in the red book***

How is a prepositional phrase used as an adverb?

A prepositional phrase is used as an adverb when it adds to the meaning of a verb or verb phrase.

> ***In the fall,** we will buy new furniture.*
> *We bought the curtains **on Saturday**.*

PREPOSITIONS/Recognizing prepositions

BEFORE STARTING THIS EXERCISE, read Grammar Rule 48 in the Reference Guide.

PRECHECK. Find the preposition in each sentence below.
Then write that preposition on the line next to the sentence.
Check your answers at the bottom of the page.

1. For centuries, people have believed that seven is a special number. _____

2. A broken mirror might bring seven years of bad luck. _____

3. Sailors have gone exploring on the seven seas. _____

4. Some people believe in seven virtues and seven sins. _____

5. People still talk about the ancient world's seven wonders. _____

Number right: _____ *If less than 5, review the rule in the Reference Guide.*

Underline each preposition in the sentences below.

1. Bobby Fischer played his first game of chess at the age of five.

2. His older sister explained the game to him.

3. Within a few years, Fischer was playing in chess tournaments.

4. In 1958, he became the youngest grandmaster in chess history.

5. He was only 15 at the time.

6. In 1972, Fischer became the first American world champion of chess.

7. He played against champion Boris Spassky of the Soviet Union.

8. The championship match was held in Reykjavik, the capital of Iceland.

9. After three years, Fischer lost his championship title because he did
   not defend it.

10. Bobby Fischer now lives in California, not far from Los Angeles.

PREPOSITIONS/Using prepositions

BEFORE STARTING THIS EXERCISE, read Grammar Rule 48 in the Reference Guide.

On the lines below, rewrite the paragraph given on the right. Replace each *** with a preposition.

Professional wrestling sometimes attracts a variety *** unusual characters. One character who comes immediately *** mind is Gorgeous George. George used a special dye *** his hair. Then he curled his hair *** rollers. And *** a wrestling match, George always sprayed the arena *** Chanel No. 5 perfume. Another unusual contestant *** wrestling was the Masked Marvel. This man always appeared *** a big black stocking cap. The cap had two small holes *** the Marvel's eyes and a larger hole *** his mouth. Can you imagine what might have happened *** a wrestling match *** Gorgeous George and the Masked Marvel? The fans would have gotten a great show *** their money.

PREPOSITIONS/Recognizing prepositional phrases

BEFORE STARTING THIS EXERCISE, read Grammar Rule 49 in the Reference Guide.

PRECHECK. Find the prepositional phrase in each sentence below. Then write that phrase on the line next to the sentence. Check your answers at the bottom of the page.

1. Surfing began in Hawaii. _____

2. People have been surfing there for centuries. _____

3. The grandfather of modern surfing is Duke Kahanamoku. _____

4. Author Jack London called surfing "the sport of sports." _____

5. Every summer, surfers wait for the perfect wave. _____

Number right: _____ *If less than 5, review the rule in the Reference Guide.*

Underline each prepositional phrase in the sentences below.

1. The Old London Bridge was designed by a priest.

2. The bridge carried people across the Thames River in London.

3. Builders worked on the bridge for 30 years.

4. The bridge was finally finished in 1209.

5. Wooden houses and a chapel were built on it.

6. For five centuries, it was the only bridge over the Thames within London.

7. In 1839, the old bridge was replaced by a new bridge made of granite.

8. The Old London Bridge was an important part of the London scene.

9. However, you cannot see it in London anymore.

10. Some Americans bought the bridge and reconstructed it at Lake Havasu, in Arizona.

PREPOSITIONS/Using prepositional phrases

BEFORE STARTING THIS EXERCISE, read Grammar Rule 49 in the Reference Guide.

On the lines below, rewrite the paragraphs given on the right. Replace each *** with a prepositional phrase.

I overheard an odd conversation *** recently. I was sitting ***, waiting ***. A man *** pointed *** ***. "Excuse me," he said, "but you are standing ***."

"Don't be ridiculous!" the woman replied. "I am certainly not standing ***. I am merely standing ***."

The man had been polite ***. Now he shouted, "I don't really care whether you're standing *** or ***. If you don't move right now, I will call my lawyer."

Unfortunately, I never heard the end *** ***. ***, it was time ***, and I couldn't keep my friends waiting.

PREPOSITIONS/Objects of prepositions

BEFORE STARTING THIS EXERCISE, read Grammar Rule 50 in the Reference Guide.

PRECHECK. Underline the prepositional phrase in each sentence below. Then find the object of the preposition in that phrase. Write the object of the preposition on the line next to the sentence. Check your answers at the bottom of the page.

1. Amelia Bloomer gave her support and her name to bloomers. _____

2. The Braille reading system is named for its inventor, Louis Braille. _____

3. Thomas Derrick, an English hangman, gave his name to modern derricks. _____

4. The inventor of those famous crackers was named Graham. _____

5. The sandwich got its name from an English earl. _____

Number right: _____ If less than 5, review the rule in the Reference Guide.

Underline each prepositional phrase in the sentences below. Then draw a second line under the object of the preposition.

1. President Teddy Roosevelt once shook hands with 8,513 people in a single day.

2. President Zachary Taylor did not vote in his own election.

3. President Herbert Hoover gave all of his salary to charities.

4. Martin Van Buren was the first American president born in the U.S.

5. President Lyndon Johnson enjoyed serving steaks cut in the shape of his home state, Texas.

6. President John Kennedy once ate 12 bowls of chowder at a single meal.

7. President Ulysses S. Grant was arrested for speeding on his horse.

8. As a boy, President Jimmy Carter sold peanuts in his hometown.

ANSWERS 1. to bloomers, bloomers 2. for its inventor, inventor 3. to modern derricks, derricks 4. of those famous crackers, crackers 5. from an English earl, earl

PREPOSITIONS/Objects of prepositions

BEFORE STARTING THIS EXERCISE, read Grammar Rule 50 in the Reference Guide.

Finish the sentences below. On each blank line, write an object of the preposition in dark type.

1. The average oyster can make a medium-sized pearl **in** five _____ .

2. Half **of** the _____ **in** _____ can ski.

3. **For** _____ , California is the most dangerous state **in** the

   _____ .

4. **For** most _____ , shoes **on** the right _____ wear out

   faster than shoes **on** the left _____ .

5. An elephant's eyelashes may grow **to** a _____ **of** five

   _____ .

6. Spiders often rub oil **on** their _____ .

7. Your hair grows faster **in** the _____ than **in** the _____ .

8. A Monopoly game you can eat has a board made **of** _____ and houses and

   hotels made **of** _____ .

9. **In** an average _____ , scientists identify 6,000 new chemical substances.

10. No one has ever found two snowflakes **with** exactly the same _____ .

11. You can fill a teaspoon **with** 120 _____ **of** _____ .

12. Some fortune-tellers look **into** the _____ **through** a crystal

    _____ .

PREPOSITIONS/Personal pronouns and prepositional phrases

BEFORE STARTING THIS EXERCISE, read Grammar Rule 51 in the Reference Guide.

PRECHECK. Decide which of the personal pronoun forms in parentheses should be used to finish each sentence below. Then write that pronoun form on the line next to the sentence. Check your answers at the bottom of the page.

1. I first heard about the plan from (him, he). _____

2. Unfortunately, it didn't make much sense to (I, me). _____

3. However, I tried to explain it to (she, her). _____

4. Then she talked to (them, they) about it. _____

5. Now it isn't clear to any of (us, we). _____

Number right: _____ *If less than 5, review the rule in the Reference Guide.*

Finish each sentence below. Select the correct personal pronoun form from the pair given before the sentence. Then write that pronoun form on the blank line.

1. we, us   The robot's flashing eyes seemed to stare right through _____ .

2. him, he   Something or someone was standing beside _____ .

3. them, they   A hundred feet below _____ , waves crashed on the rocky shore.

4. she, her   Since that day, no one has heard from _____ .

5. I, me   The stranger had winked at _____ and disappeared.

6. they, them   Someone near _____ was calling for help.

7. us, we   Hungry vultures were circling above _____ .

8. me, I   The horrible creature was coming toward _____ .

9. he, him   A huge snake slithered up beside _____ .

PREPOSITIONS/Personal pronouns and prepositional phrases

BEFORE STARTING THIS EXERCISE, read Grammar Rule 51 in the Reference Guide.

**Rewrite the sentences below. In each prepositional phrase,
change the object of the preposition to a personal pronoun.**

1. The first award was presented to Mick Jagger.

   _____

2. That official should not have been arguing with the coaches.

   _____

3. The committee members have discussed it with the mayor.

   _____

4. All the letters from Alicia had been lost.

   _____

5. Who made the movie about Patsy Cline?

   _____

6. Secret-service agents always jogged beside President Jimmy Carter.

   _____

7. No one ever saw the portrait of Mrs. Farmingham.

   _____

8. Everybody has been talking about that new television show.

   _____

9. A few lucky people have played bridge with that famous actor.

   _____

10. Unfortunately, the prize for our family was a one-dollar bill.

    _____

PREPOSITIONS/Prepositional phrases used as adjectives

BEFORE STARTING THIS EXERCISE, read Grammar Rule 52 in the Reference Guide.

PRECHECK. In each sentence below, find the prepositional phrase used as an adjective. Then write that phrase on the line below the sentence. Check your answers at the bottom of the page.

1. The first leg of the Triple Crown is the Kentucky Derby.

_____

2. Native Dancer, the winner of almost all his races, lost the 1953 Derby.

_____

3. The winning horse in the 1929 Derby had the same name as its trainer.

_____

4. Eddie Arcaro and Bill Hartack were each winning jockeys in five Derby races.

_____

5. In 1973, the colt Secretariat broke the Derby record of two minutes.

_____

Number right: _____ *If less than 5, review the rule in the Reference Guide.*

Finish each sentence below. Fill in the blank with a prepositional phrase used as an adjective.

1. No one could find the key _____ .

2. The solution _____ will be printed tomorrow.

3. The judge _____ was very strict.

4. That famous dancer actually created a ballet _____ .

5. The stars _____ are going on a nationwide tour.

PREPOSITIONS/Prepositional phrases used as adverbs

BEFORE STARTING THIS EXERCISE, read Grammar Rule 53 in the Reference Guide.

PRECHECK. In each sentence below, find the prepositional phrase used as an adverb. Then write that phrase on the line next to the sentence. Check your answers at the bottom of the page.

1. Bananas don't really grow on trees. _____

2. Eelgrass is a plant that grows under ice. _____

3. Most seaweeds are loaded with vitamins. _____

4. The first pineapples weren't grown in Hawaii. _____

5. Banana oil does not come from bananas. _____

Number right: _____ If less than 5, review the rule in the Reference Guide.

Finish the sentences below. In each blank space, write a prepositional phrase used as an adverb.

1. Suddenly, the other hikers disappeared _____ .

2. _____ , the Jets scored.

3. Thousands of fans were waiting _____ .

4. _____ , five yellow parachutes floated silently _____ .

5. _____ , the box exploded.

6. _____ , the tourists walked happily _____ .

7. _____ , Jerome and his friends had been talking _____ .

PREPOSITIONS/Prepositional phrases used as adjectives or as adverbs

BEFORE STARTING THIS EXERCISE, read Grammar Rules 52 and 53 in the Reference Guide.

PRECHECK. Underline the prepositional phrase in each sentence below. Then, on the line next to the sentence, write *adjective* if the prepositional phrase is used as an adjective. Write *adverb* if the phrase is used as an adverb. Check your answers at the bottom of the page.

1. Alice saw a white rabbit with pink eyes. _____

2. The rabbit was talking to himself. _____

3. The watch in the rabbit's paw surprised Alice. _____

4. She followed the rabbit across a field. _____

5. The rabbit led Alice into Wonderland. _____

Number right: _____ *If less than 5, review the rules in the Reference Guide.*

Underline the prepositional phrase in each sentence below. Then, on the line next to the sentence, write *adjective* if the prepositional phrase is used as an adjective. Write *adverb* if the phrase is used as an adverb.

1. Rocky and Bullwinkle live in Frostbite Falls. _____

2. Elizabeth Taylor was married to Richard Burton two times. _____

3. The first host of that game show was Art Fleming. _____

4. Dorothy and the Wizard first met in the Emerald City. _____

5. Edgar Bergen was the voice of several famous dummies. _____

6. Some original Mouseketeers are still in show business. _____

7. Groucho Marx was the star of that TV quiz show. _____

8. The original title of that movie was <u>Shirley</u>, not <u>Tootsie</u>. _____

PREPOSITIONS/Prepositional phrases used as adjectives or as adverbs

BEFORE STARTING THIS EXERCISE, read Grammar Rules 52 and 53 in the Reference Guide.

Rewrite the sentences below. Replace each *** with a prepositional phrase used as an adjective. Replace each +++ with a prepositional phrase used as an adverb.

1. The creators *** have been working +++.

_____

_____

2. The huge old home *** was sold +++.

_____

_____

3. Another guide led the group *** +++.

_____

_____

4. All the performers *** have been practicing +++.

_____

_____

5. Just then, a fish *** jumped up and landed +++.

_____

_____

6. +++, the winner *** fainted.

_____

_____

7. Everybody *** has been invited +++.

_____

_____

Writing Activity 7

If you need help, review page 107 and the rules noted on pages 108–119.

Look at the picture given on the right.

List at least six prepositions that can help you describe where things are in the closet.

_____

_____

Now, finish this paragraph about the picture. Be sure to use all of the prepositions you noted above to help you describe where things are in the closet.

The closet was a terrible mess! _____

_____

_____

_____

_____

_____

_____

_____

Previewing SENTENCE PARTS

What is a simple subject?

The simple subject of a sentence is the most important noun or pronoun in the subject.

> *Downhill **skiing** is a popular sport.*
>
> *Even young **children** can learn to ski well.*

What is a simple predicate?

The simple predicate of a sentence is the verb or verb phrase.

> *Skiing **can be** a dangerous sport.*
>
> *Skiers **hope** for lots of snow.*

What is a direct object?

A direct object is a word that tells who or what receives the action of the verb.

> *Skiers use two **ski poles.***
>
> *Sporting goods stores sell **ski boots.***

What is an indirect object?

An indirect object is a word that tells to whom or for whom the action of the verb is done.

> *The ski instructor gave **us** directions.*
>
> *She gave her **friend** a new pair of ski gloves.*

What is a predicate nominative?

A predicate nominative is a word that follows a linking verb and renames the sentence subject.

> *The winner of the race was **Eric.***
>
> *If you had raced, you would have been the **winner**.*

SENTENCE PARTS/Simple subjects

BEFORE STARTING THIS EXERCISE, read Grammar Rule 54 in the Reference Guide.

PRECHECK. Find the simple subject in each sentence below.
Then write that noun or pronoun on the line next to the
sentence. Check your answers at the bottom of the page.

1. Young seals must be taught to swim. _____

2. Pigs can get sunburned. _____

3. They should be protected from the sun. _____

4. A talented flea can jump 13 inches. _____

5. Killer whales very rarely kill people. _____

Number right: _____ *If less than 5, review the rule in the Reference Guide.*

Finish each sentence below by writing a simple subject on
the blank line.

1. The average _____ gets 140 colds in a lifetime.

2. _____ almost never falls in Lima, Peru.

3. The _____ at the South Pole is about one and a half miles deep.

4. The frightened and angry _____ stampeded.

5. Not all _____ bite people.

6. _____ had been stung by a swarm of bees.

7. Some _____ are bald.

8. Nearly all _____ get lonely.

9. A few _____ can communicate with sign language.

10. That funny-looking _____ changes colors when excited.

SENTENCE PARTS/Simple predicates

BEFORE STARTING THIS EXERCISE, read Grammar Rule 55 in the Reference Guide.

PRECHECK.   Find the simple predicate in each sentence below. Then write that verb or verb phrase on the line next to the sentence. Check your answers at the bottom of the page.

1. The last dodo bird died in 1681. _____

2. Chickens eat faster in groups than alone. _____

3. A large hippopotamus might open its mouth about four feet. _____

4. No dog can hear the lowest note on a piano. _____

5. A hog has better eyesight than a human being. _____

Number right: _____ *If less than 5, review the rule in the Reference Guide.*

Finish each sentence below by writing a simple predicate on the blank line.

1. Somebody _____ the diamonds.

2. An ostrich _____ .

3. During your lifetime, you _____ on the phone for a total of about two years.

4. Everybody _____ at least once.

5. Each contestant _____ for half an hour.

6. Then the pitcher _____ at the catcher.

7. Only a few adults _____ rock music.

8. The children _____ to go to the zoo.

9. She certainly _____ horror movies!

10. Sylvester Stallone _____ every day.

ANSWERS 1. died 2. eat 3. might open 4. can hear 5. has

123

SENTENCE PARTS/Direct objects

BEFORE STARTING THIS EXERCISE, read Grammar Rule 56 in the Reference Guide.

PRECHECK. Find the direct object in each sentence below. Then write that word on the line next to the sentence. Check your answers at the bottom of the page.

1. A Dutch scientist made the first telescope. _____

2. An undertaker invented telephones with dials. _____

3. Thomas Edison did not actually invent lightbulbs. _____

4. Mathematicians in India actually invented Arabic numbers. _____

5. Chester Greenwood made the first earmuffs in 1877. _____

Number right: _____ *If less than 5, review the rule in the Reference Guide.*

Underline the direct object in each sentence below.

1. Samoans, not Hawaiians, wore the first grass skirts.

2. Most Eskimos have never seen an igloo.

3. A cowboy's high boots protect him from snakes and burrs.

4. Many sailors have superstitions about the albatross.

5. The average American adult has seven credit cards.

6. Many secretaries do not eat lunch on weekdays.

7. Russian scientists have made new medicines out of garlic.

8. During William Shakespeare's time, no one used forks.

9. A tankful of tropical fish can soothe patients in a doctor's waiting room.

10. The employees of McDonald's take classes at Hamburger University.

ANSWERS 1. telescope 2. telephones 3. lightbulbs 4. numbers 5. earmuffs

SENTENCE PARTS/Direct objects

BEFORE STARTING THIS EXERCISE, read Grammar Rule 56 in the Reference Guide.

Rewrite the sentences below. Replace each *** with a direct-object noun.

1. The inventor had created a ***.

   _____

2. Everyone else in the room recognized our ***.

   _____

3. Dr. West attended a *** in Los Angeles.

   _____

4. Our neighbors have a *** every summer.

   _____

5. The president has just signed the ***.

   _____

6. Thousands of people have already bought their ***.

   _____

7. The thieves had not left any ***.

   _____

8. In a short race, a giraffe can outrun a ***.

   _____

9. That woman is suing her *** for five million dollars.

   _____

10. An insect cannot close its ***.

   _____

SENTENCE PARTS/Personal pronouns as direct objects

BEFORE STARTING THIS EXERCISE, read Grammar Rule 56 in the Reference Guide.

PRECHECK. Decide which of the personal pronoun forms in parentheses should be used to finish each sentence below. Then write that pronoun form on the line next to the sentence. Check your answers at the bottom of the page.

1. That team has chosen (she, her) as its new captain. _____

2. Our team elected (him, he) last month. _____

3. The members of their team do not like (we, us) very much. _____

4. We beat (them, they) in the championship game. _____

5. You should have seen (I, me) during that game! _____

Number right: _____ *If less than 5, review the rule in the Reference Guide.*

Finish each sentence below. Select the correct personal pronoun form from the pair given before the sentence. Then write that word on the blank line.

1. we, us   Somebody must have been following _____ .

2. her, she   Two talent scouts have been watching _____ in every performance.

3. he, him   No one has seen _____ all week.

4. they, them   Tessa should have phoned _____ last night.

5. me, I   Fortunately, my friends have been helping _____ .

6. him, he   Then the director tapped _____ on the shoulder.

7. us, we   Finally, Jenny told _____ about the change in plans.

8. she, her   Ralph claimed he would send _____ to the moon.

9. them, they   It'll be a while before I give _____ another chance.

10. I, me   My boss asked _____ to run an errand at lunchtime.

SENTENCE PARTS/Indirect objects

BEFORE STARTING THIS EXERCISE, read Grammar Rule 57 in the Reference Guide.

PRECHECK.   Find the indirect object in each sentence below. Then write that word on the line next to the sentence. Check your answers at the bottom of the page.

1. The committee sent every family a questionnaire. _____

2. It asked the citizens some important questions. _____

3. Several people handed the mayor their answers. _____

4. The mayor told us the history of the poll. _____

5. The poll's results have given the council some good ideas. _____

Number right: _____ *If less than 5, review the rule in the Reference Guide.*

Underline the indirect object in each sentence below.

1. Tom may have given you some good advice.

2. Her friends bought Tina a going-away present.

3. These new results will teach those politicians an important lesson.

4. That big company promises every customer complete satisfaction.

5. The artist handed the rich collector several sketches.

6. Usually the designer shows the builder all the blueprints.

7. We left Clyde a long message on his answering machine.

8. She wrote him three long letters during the weekend.

9. Carol buys herself one big present every year.

10. No one has ever sent me a dozen red roses.

SENTENCE PARTS/Indirect objects

BEFORE STARTING THIS EXERCISE, read Grammar Rule 57 in the Reference Guide.

Rewrite the sentences below. Replace each *** with an indirect-object noun.

1. Maya sent her *** a tape of the new album.

   _____

2. Unfortunately, none of us gave the *** a tip.

   _____

3. Mel is giving his *** a surprise party.

   _____

4. You probably can't teach your old *** new tricks.

   _____

5. The judge gave the *** a stern warning.

   _____

6. Then the spy handed the *** four new photographs.

   _____

7. You should have told your *** the truth.

   _____

8. They offered each *** a rather simple choice.

   _____

9. The coach wished all the *** good luck.

   _____

10. The criminal had actually left the *** a note.

    _____

SENTENCE PARTS/Personal pronouns as indirect objects

BEFORE STARTING THIS EXERCISE, read Grammar Rule 57 in the Reference Guide.

PRECHECK. Decide which of the personal pronoun forms in parentheses should be used to finish each sentence below. Then write that pronoun form on the line next to the sentence. Check your answers at the bottom of the page.

1. Claire told (we, us) the story of her secret adventure. _____

2. I probably should not have told (them, they) Claire's story. _____

3. They certainly should not have told (he, him) the story. _____

4. I had given (her, she) my word about the secret. _____

5. Now no one will tell (I, me) any more secrets. _____

Number right: _____ *If less than 5, review the rule in the Reference Guide.*

Finish each sentence below. Select the correct personal pronoun form from the pair before the sentence. Then write that word on the blank line.

1. him, he   No one had sent _____ an invitation.

2. she, her   The agents have offered _____ a better contract.

3. us, we   Nobody can make _____ three new costumes that quickly.

4. I, me   The officer showed _____ his badge.

5. her, she   Perhaps the secretary did not give _____ the message.

6. they, them   The news had clearly given _____ a shock.

7. we, us   That company sold _____ a dangerous product.

8. he, him   The flight attendant left _____ a pillow and a blanket.

9. me, I   The interviewer asked _____ some difficult questions.

10. them, they   Someone sent _____ a message in a bottle.

SENTENCE PARTS/Predicate nominatives

BEFORE STARTING THIS EXERCISE, read Grammar Rule 58 in the Reference Guide.

PRECHECK. Find the predicate nominative in each sentence below. Then write that word on the line next to the sentence. Check your answers at the bottom of the page.

1. All elephants are vegetarians. _____

2. Koalas are not bears. _____

3. Dr. D. Tortora is a psychologist for animals. _____

4. Harvey was a very famous rabbit. _____

5. A liger is a cross between a lion and a tiger. _____

Number right: _____ *If less than 5, review the rule in the Reference Guide.*

Underline the predicate nominative in each sentence below.

1. Dale Evans's horse was Buttermilk.

2. One of Michael Jackson's pets is a llama.

3. The silent member of the Marx brothers was Harpo.

4. The youngest Beatle was George Harrison.

5. Mary Tyler Moore was the star of her own television show.

6. Jack is the most common name in nursery rhymes.

7. Frank Oz is the voice of Miss Piggy.

8. The real name of singer Tiny Tim is Herbert Khaury.

9. Birchwood Elementary is the neighborhood school for Charlie Brown and his friends.

10. Bugs Bunny's buddy is Elmer Fudd.

SENTENCE PARTS/Predicate nominatives

BEFORE STARTING THIS EXERCISE, read Grammar Rule 58 in the Reference Guide.

Rewrite the sentences below. Replace each * with a
predicate nominative.**

1. That actor probably should have been a ***.

   _____

2. In my opinion, the movie was a ***.

   _____

3. Jeff was the *** in the last game.

   _____

4. Ice cream is a popular *** throughout the world.

   _____

5. Chinese checkers is actually an English ***.

   _____

6. Those green plants must be ***.

   _____

7. He is a very good ***.

   _____

8. Your funny bone is not really a ***.

   _____

9. She will probably become a famous ***.

   _____

10. Unfortunately, I am not a good ***.

   _____

Writing Activity 8

If you need help, review page 121 and the rules noted on pages 122–131.

What is your favorite game or sport? _____

On the lines below, write one or two paragraphs explaining how to play it. Try to include sentences with direct objects, indirect objects, and predicate nominatives.

_____

_____

_____

_____

_____

_____

_____

_____

_____

_____

_____

_____

_____

_____

_____

_____

_____

_____

_____

_____

_____

POSTTEST

Read each group of words below. Is it a complete sentence? Fill in the oval next to the correct letter.

1. Fleas cannot fly.

   0 A. A complete sentence
   0 B. Not a complete sentence

2. Jump a very long distance, however.

   0 A. A complete sentence
   0 B. Not a complete sentence

Read each sentence below. What kind of sentence is it? Fill in the oval next to the correct letter.

3. Which word do you say most often?

   0 A. declarative
   0 B. interrogative
   0 C. imperative
   0 D. exclamatory

4. Most people say "I" more than any other word.

   0 A. declarative
   0 B. interrogative
   0 C. imperative
   0 D. exclamatory

5. How silly people are!

   0 A. declarative
   0 B. interrogative
   0 C. imperative
   0 D. exclamatory

In the sentences below, which word or group of words identifies the subject of the sentence? Fill in the oval next to the correct letter.

6. A newborn giraffe is almost six feet tall.

   0 A. A newborn giraffe
   0 B. A newborn
   0 C. giraffe is almost
   0 D. six feet tall

7. It may grow to a height of 20 feet.

   0 A. 20 feet
   0 B. It may grow
   0 C. It
   0 D. to a height of 20 feet

In the sentences below, which word or group of words identifies the predicate of the sentence? Fill in the oval next to the correct letter.

8. I could hardly hear you.

   0 A. I
   0 B. I could
   0 C. hear you
   0 D. could hardly hear you

9. Please repeat that.

   0 A. Please
   0 B. repeat that
   0 C. Please repeat that
   0 D. Please that

Read each sentence below. Does it have a compound subject? Does it have a compound predicate? Is it a compound sentence? Fill in the oval next to the correct letter.

10. The second-highest mountain in the world was first measured in 1856, but no one succeeded in climbing it until 1954.

    0 A. compound subject
    0 B. compound predicate
    0 C. compound sentence

11. John Beresford Tipton and his secretary gave away money on the TV show <u>The Millionaire</u>.

    0 A. compound subject
    0 B. compound predicate
    0 C. compound sentence

12. Sandy Koufax struck out 2,396 batters and allowed only 1,754 hits.

    0 A. compound subject
    0 B. compound predicate
    0 C. compound sentence

Think about the underlined word or phrase in each sentence below. Which name identifies that kind of word or phrase? Fill in the oval next to the correct letter.

13. That <u>hotel</u> has 3,200 rooms.

    0 A. noun
    0 B. verb
    0 C. adjective
    0 D. adverb

14. That huge hotel is in <u>Moscow</u>.

    0 A. plural noun
    0 B. proper noun
    0 C. noun of address
    0 D. appositive noun

15. Well, <u>Dr. Watson</u>, what do you think?

    0 A. plural noun
    0 B. possessive noun
    0 C. noun of address
    0 D. appositive noun

16. Everyone wanted to hear the <u>adventurers'</u> tales.

    0 A. proper noun
    0 B. possessive noun
    0 C. noun of address
    0 D. appositive noun

17. The man, a well-known <u>actor</u>, caused a scandal.

    0 A. plural noun
    0 B. possessive noun
    0 C. noun of address
    0 D. appositive noun

18. The world's biggest mammal <u>is</u> the blue whale.

    0 A. action verb
    0 B. linking verb
    0 C. verb phrase
    0 D. adverb

19. Blue whales <u>swim</u> around Antarctica.

    0 A. action verb
    0 B. linking verb
    0 C. verb phrase
    0 D. adverb

20. Steven Spielberg <u>has directed</u> several hit movies.

    0 A. helping verb
    0 B. main verb
    0 C. verb phrase
    0 D. linking verb

21. An unknown will star in his next film.
- 0 A. helping verb
- 0 B. main verb
- 0 C. verb phrase
- 0 D. linking verb

22. A sailfish can swim almost 70 miles an hour.
- 0 A. helping verb
- 0 B. main verb
- 0 C. verb phrase
- 0 D. linking verb

23. Perhaps you were mistaken.
- 0 A. common noun
- 0 B. action verb
- 0 C. personal pronoun
- 0 D. linking verb

24. Jackson must have shown the code to someone.
- 0 A. personal pronoun
- 0 B. reflexive pronoun
- 0 C. demonstrative pronoun
- 0 D. indefinite pronoun

25. Does anyone know his real name?
- 0 A. demonstrative pronoun
- 0 B. possessive pronoun
- 0 C. indefinite pronoun
- 0 D. reflexive pronoun

26. Marla finished the project by herself.
- 0 A. indefinite pronoun
- 0 B. personal pronoun
- 0 C. demonstrative pronoun
- 0 D. reflexive pronoun

27. Actually, I would have chosen those.
- 0 A. possessive pronoun
- 0 B. indefinite pronoun
- 0 C. reflexive pronoun
- 0 D. demonstrative pronoun

28. Some squids have huge eyes.
- 0 A. common noun
- 0 B. action verb
- 0 C. adjective
- 0 D. adverb

29. Jack was happy when he got his raise.
- 0 A. predicate adjective
- 0 B. proper adjective
- 0 C. adverb
- 0 D. comparative form of adjective

30. The Russian sailor jumped overboard.
- 0 A. predicate adjective
- 0 B. proper adjective
- 0 C. adverb
- 0 D. superlative form of adjective

31. Silently, Jon pushed the door open.
- 0 A. linking verb
- 0 B. proper adjective
- 0 C. adverb
- 0 D. adverb used as intensifier

32. Very carefully, I unwrapped the ticking package.
- 0 A. action verb
- 0 B. proper noun
- 0 C. proper adjective
- 0 D. adverb used as an intensifier

33. Mindy did <u>not</u> get the part.

   0 A. adjective
   0 B. double negative
   0 C. adverb
   0 D. helping verb

34. <u>Oh</u>, I'm so sorry!

   0 A. subordinating conjunction
   0 B. coordinating conjunction
   0 C. interjection
   0 D. preposition

35. Nero did not actually fiddle <u>while</u> Rome burned.

   0 A. preposition
   0 B. interjection
   0 C. coordinating conjunction
   0 D. subordinating conjunction

36. She never saw him <u>or</u> talked to him.

   0 A. preposition
   0 B. coordinating conjunction
   0 C. interjection
   0 D. subordinating conjunction

37. The longest worms live <u>in</u> the ocean.

   0 A. coordinating conjunction
   0 B. preposition
   0 C. prepositional phrase used as an adjective
   0 D. prepositional phrase used as an adverb

38. A certain parrot <u>in England</u> can say nearly 1,000 words.

   0 A. subordinating conjunction
   0 B. prepositional phrase used as an adjective
   0 C. prepositional phrase used as an adverb
   0 D. interjection

39. Only two <u>explorers</u> survived the storm.

   0 A. simple subject
   0 B. simple predicate
   0 C. direct object
   0 D. predicate nominative

40. Their favorite rock star was <u>Tina Turner</u>.

   0 A. simple subject
   0 B. simple predicate
   0 C. indirect object
   0 D. predicate nominative

41. You could have given <u>me</u> a hint.

   0 A. simple subject
   0 B. direct object
   0 C. indirect object
   0 D. predicate nominative

42. Before joining the Beatles, Paul McCartney played the <u>trumpet</u>.

   0 A. simple predicate
   0 B. direct object
   0 C. indirect object
   0 D. predicate nominative

Each sentence below has a word left out. From the lettered choices that follow the sentence, choose the one that will complete the sentence correctly. Then fill in the oval next to the correct letter.

43. Every contestant will get three ___ .

   0 A. trys   0 B. tries

44. That is the ___ cartoon I have ever seen.

   0 A. funnier   0 B. funniest

45. Sandy usually swims ___ than Claire.

   0 A. faster   0 B. fastest

46. It was a secret message from ___ .

   0 A. they   0 B. them

REFERENCE GUIDE

Grammar Rules

SENTENCES

Grammar 1. Definition of a sentence

A sentence is a group of words that expresses a complete thought. Every sentence must have a subject and a predicate. (See Grammar 3–6.) Every sentence begins with a capital letter and ends with a punctuation mark.

> *That leopard has already killed 400 people.*
> *Is it still hungry?*
> *Be careful!*

Sometimes a sentence may have only one word. (See Grammar 5.)

> *Listen.   Hurry!*

Grammar 2. Kinds of sentences

There are four different kinds of sentences.

A *declarative sentence* makes a statement. A declarative sentence ends with a period.

> *A volcano in the Canary Islands is for sale.*

An *interrogative sentence* asks a question. An interrogative sentence ends with a question mark.

> *Who would want to buy a volcano?*

An *imperative sentence* gives a command. An imperative sentence ends with a period.

> *Show me the list of buyers.*

An *exclamatory sentence* expresses excitement. An exclamatory sentence ends with an exclamation point.

> *They must be crazy!*

Grammar 3. Subjects and predicates in declarative sentences

Every sentence has two main parts, the subject and the predicate. The subject names what the sentence is about. The predicate tells something about the subject.

In most declarative sentences, the subject is the first part. The predicate is the second part.

> *A famous sea captain   was often sick.*
> *He   suffered from seasickness.*

In some declarative sentences, the predicate is the first part. The subject is the second part.

> *Back and forth rolled   the captain's ship.*

Grammar 4. Subjects and predicates in interrogative sentences

Every interrogative sentence has a subject and a predicate. In some interrogative sentences, the subject is the first part. The predicate is the second part.

> *Who   solved the mystery?*
> *Which clue   was most important?*

In most interrogative sentences, part of the predicate comes before the subject. To find the subject and predicate, rearrange the words of the interrogative sentence. Use those words to make a declarative sentence. (The declarative sentence will not always sound natural, but it will help you.) The subject and predicate of the two sentences are the same.

> *Why did   the butler   lie about it?*
> *The butler   did lie about it why?*

Grammar 5. Subjects and predicates in imperative sentences

Only the predicate of an imperative sentence is spoken or written. The subject of the sentence is understood. That subject is always **you.**

> (You)   *Try an underhand serve.*
> (You)   *Please show me how to do it.*

Grammar 6. Subjects and predicates in exclamatory sentences

Every exclamatory sentence has a subject and a predicate. In most exclamatory sentences, the subject is the first part. The predicate is the second part.

> *Kotzebue Sound, Alaska,   is frozen over nearly all of the time!*

In some exclamatory sentences, part of the predicate comes before the subject.

> *What terrible weather   that city   has!*
> *(That city   has what terrible weather!)*

Grammar 7. Compound subjects in sentences

A sentence with a compound subject has two or more subjects with the same predicate.

> ***Jesse James and his brother Frank*** *were famous outlaws in the Old West.*
> ***Cole Younger, James Younger, and Robert Younger*** *were all members of the James gang.*

Grammar 8. Compound predicates in sentences

A sentence with a compound predicate has two or more predicates with the same subject.

> *The postal workers **took in the tailless cat and named him Kojak.***
> *Kojak **lives in the post office, catches mice, and earns a salary.***

Grammar 9. Compound sentences

A compound sentence is made up of two shorter sentences joined by a coordinating conjunction. (See Grammar 45.) A compound sentence has a subject and a predicate followed by another subject and another predicate.

> *G. David Howard set a record in 1978, and it remains unbroken.*
> *Howard told jokes for more than 13 hours, but not all of them were funny.*

NOUNS

Grammar 10. Definition of a noun

A noun is a word that names a person, a place, or a thing.

> *That brave **man** crossed the **ocean** in a **rowboat**.*

Grammar 11. Singular and plural forms of nouns

Almost every noun has two forms. The singular form names one person, place, or thing.

> *Only one **worker** in that **factory** can name the secret **ingredient**.*

The plural form names more than one person, place, or thing.

> *Several **workers** in those two **factories** can name the secret **ingredients**.*

Grammar 12. Spelling plural forms of nouns

For most nouns, add **s** to the singular form to make the plural form.

> *joke—jokes   character—characters*
> *cartoon—cartoons*

If the singular form ends in **s, ss, sh, ch,** or **x,** add **es.**

> *bus—buses   witch—witches*
> *kiss—kisses   fox—foxes*
> *wish—wishes*

If the singular form ends in a consonant and **y,** change the **y** to **i** and add **es.**

> *spy—spies   discovery—discoveries*
> *mystery—mysteries*

If the singular form ends in **f,** usually change the **f** to **v** and add **es.** If the singular form ends in **fe,** usually change the **f** to **v** and add **s.** There are some important exceptions to these rules. Look in a dictionary if you are not sure of the correct plural form.

> *half—halves   wife—wives*
> *loaf—loaves   knife—knives*

Some exceptions:

> *roof—roofs   chief—chiefs   safe—safes*

If the singular form ends in **o,** add **s** to some words and **es** to others. Look in a dictionary if you are not sure of the correct plural form.

> *studio—studios   tomato—tomatoes*
> *piano—pianos   zero—zeroes*

Some nouns change in other ways to make the plural form.

child—children   mouse—mice
woman—women   goose—geese

A few nouns have the same singular form and plural form.

sheep—sheep   deer—deer   moose—moose

Grammar 13. Proper nouns and common nouns

A proper noun is the special name of a particular person, place, or thing. Each word in a proper noun begins with a capital letter.

*Then **Max** stopped in **Junctionville** and ate a **Big Mac**.*

A common noun is the name of any person, place, or thing.

*Then the **man** stopped in a small **town** and ate a **hamburger**.*

Grammar 14. Possessive nouns

The possessive form of a noun shows ownership. Usually the possessive form of a noun is made by adding an apostrophe and **s**. (See Punctuation 20.)

*A **piranha's** teeth are as sharp as razors.*

The possessive form of a plural noun that ends in **s** is made by adding only an apostrophe. (See Punctuation 20.)

*Nobody believed the **explorers'** story.*

Grammar 15. Nouns of address

A noun of address names the person being spoken to. One or two commas separate a noun of address from the rest of a sentence. (See Punctuation 9.)

*Where are you going, **Ricky?***
*I told you, **Lucy,** that I have a rehearsal tonight.*

Grammar 16. Appositive nouns

An appositive noun renames or identifies the noun that comes before it in a sentence. An appositive noun is usually part of a group of words. The whole group of words is called an appositive. One or two commas separate an appositive from the rest of a sentence. (See Punctuation 10.)

*A Ford was the preferred car of John Dillinger, **the famous gangster**.*

*Even his sister, **the president of her own company**, would not hire him.*

VERBS

Grammar 17. Definition of a verb

A verb is a word that expresses action or being.

*The volcano **erupted** suddenly.*
*It **was** a terrific surprise.*

Almost all verbs have different forms to show differences in time.

*Sometimes puffs of smoke **rise** from the volcano.*
*A huge cloud of heavy gray smoke **rose** from it last week.*

Grammar 18. Action verbs

Most verbs are action verbs. An action verb expresses physical action or mental action.

*The committee members **banned** Donald Duck comic books.*
*They **disliked** the duck's behavior.*

Grammar 19. Linking verbs

Some verbs are linking verbs. A linking verb tells what the sentence subject is or is like. The most common linking verb is **be**. (See Grammar 23.)

*A black and white dog **became** a mail carrier in California.*
*The dog's name **was** Dorsey.*

Grammar 20. Verb phrases

A verb phrase is made up of two or more verbs that function together in a sentence. The final verb in a verb phrase is the main verb.

*The 13,000-pound bell **had disappeared**.*

*Somebody **must have stolen** it.*

The verbs before the main verb in a verb phrase are helping verbs. The most common helping verbs are forms of **be** (**is, are, am, was, were**), forms of **have** (**has, have, had**), and forms of **do** (**does, do, did**). (See Grammar 23.)

*That radio station **is sponsoring** a contest.*
*The station **has** already **received** 45,217 postcards.*

Grammar 21. Agreement of verbs with nouns

Verbs that express continuing action or existence and verbs that express current action or existence are in the present tense. Almost all present-tense verbs have two different forms. These two different forms go with different sentence subjects. The verb in a sentence, or the first helping verb in a sentence, must agree with the most important word in the subject of that sentence.

One present-tense form of a verb agrees with singular nouns. This verb form ends with **s.**

> A tick **sucks** blood from larger animals.

The other present-tense form of a verb agrees with plural nouns.

> Ticks **suck** blood from larger animals.

Grammar 22. Agreement of verbs with compound subjects

The present-tense verb form that agrees with plural nouns also agrees with compound subjects. (See Grammar 7.)

> Beth Obermeyer and her daughter Kristen **hold** a record for long-distance tap dancing.

Grammar 23. Forms of the verb *be*

The verb **be** has more forms than other verbs. **Be** has three present-tense forms: **is, are,** and **am. Is** agrees with singular nouns. **Are** agrees with plural nouns. **Am** agrees with the pronoun **I.**

> Mary Lou Retton **is** a famous gymnast.
> Many people **are** her fans.
> I **am** a pretty good gymnast, too.

Most verbs have one past-tense form that tells about action or existence in the past. **Be** has two past-tense forms: **was** and **were. Was** agrees with singular noun subjects. **Were** agrees with plural noun subjects.

> The argument **was** noisy.
> Several neighbors **were** very angry about it.

Grammar 24. Irregular verbs

Usually the past-tense form of a verb ends in **d** or **ed.**

> William Baxter **invented** an important part of the Morse code.

Some verbs change in other ways to form the past tense. These are called *irregular* verbs. Look in a dictionary if you are not sure of the correct past-tense form of a verb.

> Samuel Morse **took** all the credit.

PRONOUNS

Grammar 25. Personal pronouns

A personal pronoun is a word that takes the place of one or more nouns.

> Superman tried to enlist in the Army during World War II, but **he** was found unfit to serve.

Grammar 26. Subject forms and object forms of personal pronouns

Each personal pronoun has a subject form and an object form. These different forms are used in different ways in sentences. (The pronouns **it** and **you** are the same in the subject form and the object form.) These are the subject forms of personal pronouns: **I, you, he, she, it, we, they.** These are the object forms of personal pronouns: **me, you, him, her, it, us, them.**

> **He** saw through a wall and read the wrong eye chart.
> The army did not accept **him.**

Grammar 27. Antecedents of pronouns

A personal pronoun refers to the noun it replaces. That noun is the antecedent of the pronoun.

> **Roy Rogers** became famous in movies. **He** was usually accompanied by his horse, Trigger, and his dog, Bullet.

If a personal pronoun takes the place of two or more nouns, those nouns together are the antecedent of the pronoun.

> **Roy Rogers and Dale Evans** often worked together. **They** made dozens of movies.

Grammar 28. Subject-verb agreement with personal pronouns

The present-tense verb form that agrees with singular nouns also agrees with the pronoun subjects **he, she,** and **it.**

> She **tests** new planes.

The present-tense verb form that agrees with plural nouns also agrees with the pronoun subjects **I, you, we,** and **they.**

> They **test** new planes.

Grammar 29.   Indefinite pronouns

A word that refers to a general group but does not have a specific antecedent is an indefinite pronoun.

> *Nobody can be right about everything.*

One common indefinite pronoun, **no one**, is written as two words.

Grammar 30.   Subject-verb agreement with indefinite pronouns

The present-tense verb form that agrees with singular nouns also agrees with most indefinite pronouns.

> *Almost everyone remembers the Alamo.*
> *No one knows exactly what happened there.*
> *Of the accounts written of the battle, several claim to be factual.*

Grammar 31.   Possessive pronouns

A personal pronoun that shows ownership is a possessive pronoun.

These possessive pronouns are used before nouns in sentences: **my, your, his, her, its, our, their.**

> *Why are my gym shoes in your locker?*

These possessive pronouns stand alone in sentences: **mine, yours, his, hers, its, ours, theirs.**

> *Are these gym shoes mine, or are they yours?*

Unlike possessive nouns, possessive pronouns are not written with apostrophes.

Grammar 32.   Reflexive pronouns

A pronoun that refers back to a noun or pronoun in the same sentence is a reflexive pronoun. These words are reflexive pronouns: **myself, yourself, himself, herself, itself, ourselves, yourselves, themselves.**

> *The witness had been talking to himself.*
> *You should have bought yourself a ticket.*

Grammar 33.   Demonstrative pronouns

A word that points out one or more people or things is a demonstrative pronoun. These four words can be demonstrative pronouns: **this, that, these,** and **those.**

> *These are the funniest cartoons.*
> *Nobody laughed at those.*

If the word **this, that, these,** or **those** is followed by a noun, the word is not a demonstrative pronoun. (See Grammar 34.)

ADJECTIVES

Grammar 34.   Definition of an adjective

A word that adds to the meaning of a noun or pronoun is an adjective. Adjectives usually tell what kind, which one, or how many.

> *Those exhausted men have been playing tennis for nine hours.*

Adjectives that tell what kind can sometimes stand alone.

> *They were exhausted.*

Adjectives that tell which one or how many always come before nouns.

> *Both players have used several rackets.*

Grammar 35.   The adjectives *a* and *an*

The adjectives **a** and **an** are usually called *indefinite articles.* (The adjective **the** is usually called a *definite article.*) **A** is used before words that begin with consonants or with a "yew" sound.

> *A penguin cannot fly.*
> *Cooking is a useful activity.*

An is used before words that begin with vowels or with an unsounded **h.**

> *An ostrich cannot fly.*
> *Brutus is an honorable man.*

Grammar 36.   Predicate adjectives

An adjective that comes after a linking verb and adds to the meaning of the subject noun or pronoun is a predicate adjective.

> *Maria Spelterina must have been brave.*
> *Her tightrope walks across Niagara Falls were dangerous.*

Grammar 37.   Proper adjectives

An adjective that is formed from a proper noun is a proper adjective. Each word in a proper adjective begins with a capital letter.

> *The American dollar is worth less than the British pound.*
> *The new Spielberg film is great!*

Grammar 38.   Comparative and superlative forms of adjectives

Adjectives can be used to compare two or more people or things. When only two people or things are compared, use the comparative form of an adjective. To make the comparative form, add **er** to adjectives with one syllable and many adjectives with two syllables. Use **more** (or **less**) before some adjectives with two syllables and all adjectives with more than two syllables. Look in a dictionary if you are not sure of the correct comparative form of an adjective.

> *Buster Keaton was **funnier** than Charlie Chaplin.*
>
> *Buster Keaton was **more amusing** than Charlie Chaplin.*

When more than two people or things are compared, use the superlative form of an adjective. To make the superlative form, add **est** to adjectives with one syllable and many adjectives with two syllables. Use **most** (or **least**) before some adjectives with two syllables and all adjectives with more than two syllables. Look in a dictionary if you are not sure of the correct superlative form of an adjective.

> *Buster Keaton was the **funniest** movie actor who ever lived.*
>
> *Buster Keaton was the **most amusing** movie actor who ever lived.*

The comparative and superlative forms of the adjective **good** are **better** and **best**.

> *Buster Keaton was a **better** actor than Charlie Chaplin.*
>
> *Buster Keaton was the **best** movie actor who ever lived.*

The comparative and superlative forms of the adjective **bad** are **worse** and **worst**.

> *The Revenge of the Killer Tomatoes was a **worse** movie than The Fly.*
>
> *The Revenge of the Killer Tomatoes was probably the **worst** movie ever made.*

ADVERBS

Grammar 39. Definition of an adverb

A word that adds to the meaning of a verb or verb phrase is an adverb. Adverbs usually tell where, when, how, or how often.

> *The rodeo rider **bravely** mounted the mustang **again**.*

Grammar 40. Comparative and superlative forms of adverbs

Adverbs can be used to compare the actions of two or more people or things.

When only two people or things are compared, use the comparative form of an adverb. To make the comparative form, usually use **more** (or **less**) before the adverb. Add **er** to a few short adverbs.

> *Polly speaks **more clearly** than that other parrot.*
>
> *Polly can fly **higher** than that other parrot.*

When more than two people or things are compared, use the superlative form of an adverb. To make the superlative form, usually use **most** (or **least**) before the adverb. Add **est** to a few short adverbs.

> *Of all those parrots, Polly speaks **most clearly**.*
>
> *Of all those parrots, Polly can fly **highest**.*

The comparative and superlative forms of the adverb **well** are **better** and **best**.

> *That parrot behaved **better** than your pet cat.*
>
> *Of all the unusual pets in the show, the parrot behaved **best**.*

The comparative and superlative forms of the adverb **badly** are **worse** and **worst**.

> *Your pet monkey behaved **worse** than that parrot.*
>
> *Of all the unusual pets in the show, your cat behaved **worst**.*

Grammar 41. Using adjectives and adverbs

Use an adjective to add to the meaning of a noun or a pronoun.

> *The **proud** actor accepted the prize.*

Use an adverb to add to the meaning of a verb or a verb phrase. Many (but not all) adverbs end in **ly**.

> *The actor accepted the prize **proudly**.*

Grammar 42. The adverb *not*

The adverb **not** changes the meaning of the verb or verb phrase in a sentence.

> *The soldiers in the fort would **not** surrender.*
>
> *Help did **not** arrive in time.*

Grammar 43. Avoiding double negatives

The adverb **not** is a negative word. Other common negative words are **no, never, no one, nobody, nothing, nowhere, hardly, barely,** and **scarcely.** Use only one negative word to make a sentence mean **no** or **not**.

> ***No one** ever understands how I feel.*
>
> *My friends **never** understand how I feel.*
>
> ***Hardly** anyone understands how I feel.*

Grammar 44. Adverbs used as intensifiers

Certain adverbs add to the meaning of adjectives or other adverbs. These special adverbs are sometimes called *intensifiers*.

> One **terribly** nosy neighbor heard the whole conversation.
>
> **Very** nervously, she told the police all about it.

CONJUNCTIONS

Grammar 45. Coordinating conjunctions

A word used to join two equal parts of a sentence is a coordinating conjunction. The most common coordinating conjunctions are **and, but,** and **or.**

> Many people have driven across the country, **but** these two men did it the hard way.
>
> Charles Creighton **and** James Hargis drove across the country **and** back again.
>
> They never stopped the engine **or** took the car out of reverse gear.

Grammar 46. Subordinating conjunctions and complex sentences

A word used to begin an adverb clause is a subordinating conjunction. The most common subordinating conjunctions are listed below.

after	before	though	when
although	if	unless	whenever
because	since	until	while

An adverb clause is a group of words that has a subject and a predicate but that cannot stand alone as a sentence. An adverb clause functions like an adverb. It tells when, where, how, or why. An adverb clause usually comes at the end or at the beginning of a sentence. (See Punctuation 8.) A sentence formed from an adverb clause (which cannot stand alone) and a main clause (which can stand alone) is called a *complex sentence*.

> Otto E. Funk played his violin **while he walked from New York City to San Francisco.**
>
> **When he finished his musical journey,** both his feet and his hands were tired.
>
> **Whenever it is threatened,** an opossum plays dead.
>
> It can be poked, picked up, and even rolled over **while it remains completely rigid.**

INTERJECTIONS

Grammar 47. Definition of an interjection

A word that simply expresses emotion is an interjection. A comma or an exclamation point separates an interjection from the rest of a sentence. (See Punctuation 11.)

> **Oh,** now it makes sense.
>
> **Wow!** That's terrific news!

PREPOSITIONS

Grammar 48. Definition of a preposition

A word that shows the relationship of a noun or pronoun to some other word in a sentence is a preposition. The most common prepositions are listed below.

about	below	in	to
above	beneath	into	toward
across	beside	like	under
after	between	of	until
against	beyond	off	up
along	by	on	upon
among	down	over	with
around	during	past	within
at	except	since	without
before	for	through	
behind	from	throughout	

Grammar 49. Prepositional phrases

A preposition must be followed by a noun or a pronoun. The preposition and the noun or pronoun that follows it form a prepositional phrase.

> A new record **for sit-ups** was set **by Dr. David G. Jones.**
>
> His family and friends were very proud **of him.**

Often, other words come between the preposition and the noun or pronoun. Those words are also part of the prepositional phrase.

> He set a new record **for consecutive straight-legged sit-ups.**

Grammar 50. Objects of prepositions

A preposition must be followed by a noun or a pronoun. That noun or pronoun is the object of the preposition.

> One of the main **characters** of **Star Trek** didn't appear until the second **season.**

Grammar 51. Personal pronouns in prepositional phrases

A personal pronoun that is the object of a preposition should be in the object form. These are object-form pronouns: **me, you, him, her, it, us, them.**

> The other presents for **her** are still on the table.
> The most interesting present is from **me.**

Grammar 52. Prepositional phrases used as adjectives

Some prepositional phrases are used as adjectives. They add to the meaning of a noun or pronoun in a sentence.

> The Caribbean island **of Martinique** is a department **of the French government.**

Grammar 53. Prepositional phrases used as adverbs

Some prepositional phrases are used as adverbs. They add to the meaning of the verb or verb phrase in a sentence.

> **In 1763,** Napoleon Bonaparte's wife, Josephine, was born **on Martinique.**

SENTENCE PARTS

Grammar 54. Simple subjects

The most important noun or pronoun in the subject of a sentence is the simple subject of that sentence. The object of a preposition cannot be the simple subject of a sentence.

> A 27-year-old **man** from Oklahoma swam the entire length of the Mississippi River.
> **He** spent a total of 742 hours in the river.

Grammar 55. Simple predicates

The verb or verb phrase of a sentence is the simple predicate of that sentence.

> Actor W. C. Fields **may have had** 700 separate savings accounts.
> Fields **used** a different name for each account.

Grammar 56. Direct objects

A word that tells who or what receives the action of a verb is the direct object of the verb. A direct object must be a noun or a pronoun. A personal pronoun that is a direct object should be in the object form. These are object-form pronouns: **me, you, him, her, it, us, them.**

> The first aspirin tablets contained **heroin.**
> A German company sold **them** for 12 years.

Grammar 57. Indirect objects

A word that tells to whom (or what) or for whom (or what) something is done is the indirect object of the verb expressing the action. An indirect object comes before a direct object and is not part of a prepositional phrase. An indirect object must be a noun or a pronoun. A personal pronoun that is a direct object should be in the object form. These are object-form pronouns: **me, you, him, her, it, us, them.**

> Professor Sommers gave his **students** the same lecture every year.
> He told **them** a familiar story.

Grammar 58. Predicate nominatives

A word that follows a linking verb and renames the sentence subject is the predicate nominative of a sentence. A predicate nominative must be a noun or a pronoun. A personal pronoun that is a predicate nominative should be in the subject form. These are subject-form pronouns: **I, you, he, she, it, we, they.**

> The best candidate was **Andrea.**
> In my opinion, the winner should have been **she.**

Capitalization Rules

Capitalization 1. First word in a sentence

Begin the first word in every sentence with a capital letter.

> *Who* won the eating contest?
> *That* man ate 17 bananas in two minutes.

Capitalization 2. Personal pronoun *I*

Write the pronoun **I** with a capital letter.

> At the last possible minute, *I* changed my mind.

Capitalization 3. Names and initials of people

Almost always, begin each part of a person's name with a capital letter.

> *Toby Ohara   Rosie Delancy*
> *Sue Ellen Macmillan*

Some names have more than one capital letter. Other names have parts that are not capitalized. Check the correct way to write each person's name. (Look in a reference book, or ask the person.)

> *Tim O'Hara   Tony de la Cruz*
> *Jeannie McIntyre*

Use a capital letter to write an initial that is part of a person's name.

> *B. J. Gallardo   J. Kelly Hunt*
> *John F. Kennedy*

Capitalization 4. Titles of people

Begin the title before a person's name with a capital letter.

> **Mr.** *Sam Yee*   **Captain** *Cook*
> **Dr.** *Watson*   **Governor** *Maxine Smart*

Do not use a capital letter if this kind of word is not used before a person's name.

> Did you call the **doctor?**
> Who will be our state's next **governor?**

Capitalization 5. Names of relatives

A word like **grandma** or **uncle** may be used as a person's name or as part of a person's name. Begin this kind of word with a capital letter.

> Only **Dad** and **Aunt Ellie** understand it.

Usually, if a possessive pronoun comes before a word like **grandma** or **uncle,** do not begin that word with a capital letter.

> Only **my dad** and **my aunt** understand it.

Capitalization 6. Names of days

Begin the name of a day with a capital letter.

> Most people don't have to work on **Saturday** or **Sunday.**

Capitalization 7. Names of months

Begin the name of a month with a capital letter.

> At the equator, the hottest months are **March** and **September.**

Capitalization 8. Names of holidays

Begin each important word in the name of a holiday with a capital letter. Words like **the** and **of** do not begin with capital letters.

> They usually have a picnic on the **Fourth of July** and a fancy dinner party on **Thanksgiving.**

Capitalization 9. Names of streets and highways

Begin each word in the name of a street or highway with a capital letter.

> Why is **Lombard Street** known as the most crooked road in the world?

Capitalization 10. Names of cities and towns

Begin each word in the name of a city or town with a capital letter.

> In 1957, the Dodgers moved from **Brooklyn** to **Los Angeles.**

Capitalization 11. Names of states, countries, and continents

Begin each word in the name of a state, country, or continent with a capital letter.

> The story was set in **Nevada,** but they shot the film in **Mexico.**
> There are very high mountain peaks in **Antarctica.**

Capitalization 12. Names of mountains and bodies of water

Begin each word in the name of a mountain, river, lake, or ocean with a capital letter.

*Amelia Earhart's plane was lost somewhere over the **Pacific Ocean.***

Capitalization 13. Abbreviations

If the word would begin with a capital letter, begin the abbreviation with a capital letter.

*On the scrap of paper, the victim had written, "**Wed.—Dr.** Lau."*

Capitalization 14. Titles of works

Use a capital letter to begin the first word, the last word, and every main word in the title of a work. The words **the, a,** and **an** do not begin with capital letters except at the beginning of a title. Coordinating conjunctions and prepositions also do not begin with capital letters. (See Grammar 45 and Grammar 48.)

*Archie and Edith were the main characters in the television series **All in the Family**.*

Capitalization 15. Other proper nouns

Begin each major word in a proper noun with a capital letter. A proper noun is the special name of a particular person, place, or thing. (See Grammar 13.) Usually, the words **the, a,** and **an,** coordinating conjunctions, and prepositions do not begin with capital letters. (See Grammar 45 and Grammar 48.)

*Jerry rushed to the **Burger King** and ordered three **Whoppers**.*

Capitalization 16. Proper adjectives

Begin each word in a proper adjective with a capital letter. A proper adjective is an adjective that is formed from a proper noun. (See Grammar 37.)

*That **American** author writes about **English** detectives.*
*She loves **Alfred Hitchcock** movies.*

Capitalization 17. Direct quotations

Begin the first word in a direct quotation with a capital letter. (See Punctuation 14–16.)

*Dr. Pavlik said, "**There** are simply no teeth in the denture law."*

If the words that tell who is speaking come in the middle of a quoted sentence, do not begin the second part of the quotation with a capital letter.

*"**There** are simply no teeth," said Dr. Pavlik, "**in** the denture law."*

Capitalization 18. Greetings and closings in letters

Begin the first word in the greeting of a letter with a capital letter.

***Dear** Mr. Lincoln:*   ***Dear** Uncle Abe,*

Begin the first or only word in the closing of a letter with a capital letter.

***Sincerely** yours,*   ***Very** truly yours,*
***Love**,*

Capitalization 19. Outlines

In an outline, begin the first word of each heading with a capital letter.

> II. *Houses by mail order*
>   A. *First sold by Sears, Roebuck in 1903*
>   1. *Build-it-yourself kits*
>   2. *Included all materials and instructions*
>   B. *Other companies now in business*

In an outline, use capital Roman numerals to label main ideas. Use capital letters to label supporting ideas. For ideas under supporting ideas, use Arabic numerals. For details, use small letters. Use a period after each Roman numeral, capital letter, Arabic numeral, or small letter.

> I. *Miner George Warren*
>   A. *Risked his share of Copper Queen mine in bet*
>   1. *Bet on race against George Atkins*
>   a. *Warren on foot*
>   b. *Atkins on horseback*
>   2. *Lost property worth $20 million*

Punctuation Rules

Punctuation 1. Periods, question marks, and exclamation points at the ends of sentences

Use a period, a question mark, or an exclamation point at the end of every sentence. Do not use more than one of these marks at the end of a sentence. For example, do not use both a question mark and an exclamation point, or do not use two exclamation points.

Use a period at the end of a declarative sentence (a sentence that makes a statement).

A hockey player must be able to skate backward at top speed.

Also use a period at the end of an imperative sentence (a sentence that gives a command).

Keep your eye on the puck.

Use a question mark at the end of an interrogative sentence (a sentence that asks a question).

Who is the goalie for their team?

Use an exclamation point at the end of an exclamatory sentence (a sentence that expresses excitement).

That was a terrific block!

Punctuation 2. Periods with abbreviations

Use a period at the end of each part of an abbreviation.

Most titles used before people's names are abbreviations. These abbreviations may be used in formal writing. (**Miss** is not an abbreviation and does not end with a period.)

Dr. Blackwell   *Mr. Bill Tilden*
Ms. Maureen Connolly

Most other abbreviations may be used in addresses, notes, and informal writing. They should not be used in formal writing.

Lake View Blvd.   *Mon. and Thurs.*
Fifth Ave.   *Dec. 24*

Do not use periods in the abbreviations of names of government agencies, labor unions, and certain other organizations.

Tomorrow night CBS will broadcast a special program about the FBI.

Do not use periods after two-letter state abbreviations in addresses. This special kind of abbreviation has two capital letters and no period. Use these abbreviations only in addresses.

Their new address is 1887 West Third Street, Los Angeles, CA 90048.

Punctuation 3. Periods after initials

Use a period after an initial that is part of a person's name.

Chester A. Arthur   *C. C. Pyle*
Susan B. Anthony

Punctuation 4. Commas in dates

Use a comma between the number of the day and the number of the year in a date.

Hank Aaron hit his record-breaking home run on April 8, 1974.

If the date does not come at the end of a sentence, use another comma after the number of the year.

April 8, 1974, was an exciting day for Hank Aaron's fans.

Do not use a comma in a date that has only the name of a month and the number of a year.

Aaron hit his final home run in July 1976.

Do not use a comma in a date that has only the name of a month and the number of a day.

April 8 is the anniversary of Aaron's record-breaking home run.

Punctuation 5. Commas in place names

Use a comma between the name of a city or town and the name of a state or country.

The world's largest chocolate factory is in Hershey, Pennsylvania.

If the two names do not come at the end of a sentence, use another comma after the name of the state or country.

Hershey, Pennsylvania, is the home of the world's largest chocolate factory.

Punctuation 6. Commas in compound sentences

Use a comma before the conjunction—**and, but,** or **or**—in a compound sentence. (See Grammar 9 and Grammar 45.)

*Eighteen people tried, **but** no one succeeded.*

Punctuation 7. Commas in series

Three or more words or groups of words used the same way in a sentence form a series. Use commas to separate the words or word groups in a series.

__Jamie, Mitch, Kim, Lou, and Pablo__ entered the contest.

*Each contestant **swam one mile, bicycled two miles, and ran five miles.***

Punctuation 8. Commas after introductory phrases and clauses

Use a comma after a phrase that comes before the subject of a sentence. A phrase is a group of words that usually functions as an adjective or an adverb. One kind of phrase is a prepositional phrase. (See Grammar 49.)

__In the old dresser,__ Penny found the diamonds.

If the entire predicate comes before the subject of the sentence, do not use a comma. (See Grammar 3.)

In the old dresser lay the diamonds.

Use a comma after an adverb clause at the beginning of a sentence. (See Grammar 46.)

__When he was first named hockey's most valuable player,__ Wayne Gretzky was only 18 years old.

Punctuation 9. Commas with nouns of address

Use a comma after a noun of address at the beginning of a sentence. (See Grammar 15.)

__Fernando,__ that was a terrific pitch!

Use a comma before a noun of address at the end of a sentence.

*That was a terrific pitch, **Fernando!***

If a noun of address comes in the middle of a sentence, use one comma before the noun and another comma after it.

*That, **Fernando,** was a terrific pitch!*

Punctuation 10. Commas with appositives

Use a comma before an appositive at the end of a sentence. (See Grammar 16.)

*This costume was worn by George Reeves, **Hollywood's first Superman.***

If an appositive comes in the middle of a sentence, use one comma before the appositive and another comma after it.

*George Reeves, **Hollywood's first Superman,** wore this costume.*

Punctuation 11. Commas or exclamation points with interjections

Usually, use a comma after an interjection. (See Grammar 47.)

__Well,__ we should probably think about it.

Use an exclamation point after an interjection that expresses excitement.

__Wow!__ That's a terrific idea!

Punctuation 12. Commas after greetings in friendly letters

Use a comma after the greeting in a friendly letter.

Dear John,   Dear Uncle Theodore,

Punctuation 13. Commas after closings in friendly letters and business letters

Use a comma after the closing in a letter.

Love,   Yours sincerely,

Punctuation 14. Quotation marks with direct quotations

A direct quotation tells the exact words a person said. Use quotation marks at the beginning and at the end of each part of a direct quotation.

"Look!" cried Tina. "That cat is smiling!"

"Of course," said Tom. "It's a Cheshire cat."

Punctuation 15. Commas with direct quotations

Usually, use a comma to separate the words of a direct quotation from the words that tell who is speaking. (See Punctuation 16.)

Jay asked, "Who won the game last night?"

"The Cubs won it," said Linda, "in 14 innings."

Punctuation 16. End punctuation with direct quotations

At the end of a direct quotation, use a period, a comma, a question mark, or an exclamation point before the closing quotation marks.

If the direct quotation makes a statement or gives a command at the end of a sentence, use a period.

> *Linda said, "The Cubs won last night's game."*
> *Jay said, "Tell us about the game."*

If the direct quotation makes a statement or gives a command before the end of a sentence, use a comma.

> *"The Cubs won last night's game," said Linda.*
> *"Tell us about the game," Jay said.*

If the direct quotation asks a question, use a question mark.

> *"Was it an exciting game?" asked Jay.*

If the direct quotation expresses excitement, use an exclamation point.

> *Linda yelled, "It was great!"*

Punctuation 17. Quotation marks with titles of works

Use quotation marks around the title of a story, poem, song, essay, or chapter.

> **"Happy Birthday to You"** *is the most popular song in the world.*

If a period or a comma comes after the title, put the period or comma inside the closing quotation mark.

> *The most popular song in the world is* **"Happy Birthday to You."**

Punctuation 18. Underlines with titles of works

Underline the title of a book, play, magazine, movie, television series, or newspaper.

> *One of the best movies about baseball was* **The Natural.**

Punctuation 19. Apostrophes in contractions

Use an apostrophe in place of the missing letter or letters in a contraction.

> *is not—isn't   Mel is—Mel's   I will—I'll*

Punctuation 20. Apostrophes in possessive nouns

Use an apostrophe and **s** to write the possessive form of a singular noun. (See Grammar 14.)

> *This cage belongs to one bird. It is the* **bird's** *cage.*
> *This cage belongs to Tweeter. It is* **Tweeter's** *cage.*

Use only an apostrophe to write the possessive form of a plural noun that ends in **s.**

> *This is a club for boys. It is a* **boys'** *club.*

Use an apostrophe and **s** to write the possessive form of a plural noun that does not end in **s.**

> *This is a club for men. It is a* **men's** *club.*

Punctuation 21. Colons after greetings in business letters

Use a colon after the greeting in a business letter.

> *Dear Mrs. Huan: Dear Sir or Madam:*
> *Dear Senator Rayburn:*

Punctuation 22. Colons in expressions of time

When you use numerals to write time, use a colon between the hour and the minutes.

> *5:45 P.M.   9:00 A.M.   12:17 P.M.*

Punctuation 23. Hyphens in numbers and fractions

Use a hyphen in a compound number from twenty-one to ninety-nine.

> *thirty-seven   fifty-eight   seventy-three*

Use a hyphen in a fraction.

> *one-quarter   two-thirds   seven-eighths*

Notes

Notes

Notes